T0123221

MACAT

An Analysis of

Betty Friedan's

The Feminine Mystique

Elizabeth Whitaker

Published by Macat International Ltd
24:13 Coda Centre, 189 Munster Road, London SW6 6AW.

Distributed exclusively by Routledge
2 Park Square, Milton Park, Abingdon, Oxon OX14 4RN
711 Third Avenue, New York, NY 10017, USA

Routledge is an imprint of the Taylor & Francis Group, an informa business

www.macat.com
info@macat.com

Cataloguing in Publication Data
A catalogue record for this book is available from the British Library.
Library of Congress Cataloguing-in-Publication Data is available upon request.
Cover illustration: Kim Thompson

ISBN 978-1-912303-57-1 (hardback)
ISBN 978-1-912128-88-4 (paperback)
ISBN 978-1-912282-03-6 (e-book)

Notice
The information in this book is designed to orientate readers of the work under analysis,
to elucidate and contextualise its key ideas and themes, and to aid in the development
of critical thinking skills. It is not meant to be used, nor should it be used, as a
substitute for original thinking or in place of original writing or research. References and
notes are provided for informational purposes and their presence does not constitute
endorsement of the information or opinions therein. This book is presented solely for
educational purposes. It is sold on the understanding that the publisher is not engaged
to provide any scholarly advice. The publisher has made every effort to ensure that
this book is accurate and up-to-date, but makes no warranties or representations with
regard to the completeness or reliability of the information it contains. The information
and the opinions provided herein are not guaranteed or warranted to produce particular
results and may not be suitable for students of every ability. The publisher shall not be
liable for any loss, damage or disruption arising from any errors or omissions, or from
the use of this book, including, but not limited to, special, incidental, consequential or
other damages caused, or alleged to have been caused, directly or indirectly, by the
information contained within.

CONTENTS

THE MACAT LIBRARY

The Macat Library is a series of unique academic explorations of seminal works in the humanities and social sciences – books and papers that have had a significant and widely recognised impact on their disciplines. It has been created to serve as much more than just a summary of what lies between the covers of a great book. It illuminates and explores the influences on, ideas of, and impact of that book. Our goal is to offer a learning resource that encourages critical thinking and fosters a better, deeper understanding of important ideas.

Each publication is divided into three Sections: Influences, Ideas, and Impact. Each Section has four Modules. These explore every important facet of the work, and the responses to it.

This Section-Module structure makes a Macat Library book easy to use, but it has another important feature. Because each Macat book is written to the same format, it is possible (and encouraged!) to cross-reference multiple Macat books along the same lines of inquiry or research. This allows the reader to open up interesting interdisciplinary pathways.

To further aid your reading, lists of glossary terms and people mentioned are included at the end of this book (these are indicated by an asterisk [*] throughout) – as well as a list of works cited.

Macat has worked with the University of Cambridge to identify the elements of critical thinking and understand the ways in which six different skills combine to enable effective thinking.
Three allow us to fully understand a problem; three more give us the tools to solve it. Together, these six skills make up the **PACIER** model of critical thinking. They are:

ANALYSIS – understanding how an argument is built
EVALUATION – exploring the strengths and weaknesses of an argument
INTERPRETATION – understanding issues of meaning

CREATIVE THINKING – coming up with new ideas and fresh connections
PROBLEM-SOLVING – producing strong solutions
REASONING – creating strong arguments

To find out more, visit **WWW.MACAT.COM.**

CRITICAL THINKING AND *THE FEMININE MYSTIQUE*

Primary critical thinking skill: CREATIVE THINKING
Secondary critical thinking skill: INTERPRETATION

Betty Friedan's book *The Feminine Mystique* is possibly the best-selling of all the titles analysed in the Macat library, and arguably one of the most important. Yet it was the product of an apparently minor, meaningless assignment. Undertaking to approach former classmates who had attended Smith College with her, 10 years after their graduation, the high-achieving Friedan was astonished to discover that the survey she had undertaken for a magazine feature revealed a high proportion of her contemporaries were suffering from a malaise she had thought was unique to her: profound dissatisfaction at the 'ideal' lives they had been living as wives, mothers and homemakers.

For Friedan, this discovery stimulated a remarkable burst of creative thinking, as she began to connect the elements of her own life together in new ways. The popular idea that men and women were equal, but different – that men found their greatest fulfilment through work, while women were most fulfilled in the home – stood revealed as a fallacy, and the depression and even despair she and so many other women felt as a result was recast not as a failure to adapt to a role that was the truest expression of femininity, but as the natural product of undertaking repetitive, unfulfilling and unremunerated labor.

Friedan's seminal expression of these new ideas redefined an issue central to many women's lives so successfully that it fuelled a movement – the 'second wave' feminism of the 1960s and 1970s that fundamentally challenged the legal and social framework underpinning an entire society.

ABOUT THE AUTHOR OF THE ORIGINAL WORK

Betty Friedan was born in 1921 in Illinois, United States, growing into a clever child who was already writing about politics in high school. As editor of her college newspaper, she encouraged debate about the labor movement at home and fascism in Europe.

Friedan cut short a promising academic career to become an activist and journalist in New York. When she agreed to conduct a poll of her old classmates in 1957, it revealed deep unhappiness among the nation's housewives, and inspired her best-known work, *The Feminine Mystique*. Friedan became a world-famous figure in the feminist movement and died in 2006, on her 85th birthday.

ABOUT THE AUTHOR OF THE ANALYSIS

Dr Elizabeth Whitaker holds a PhD in anthropology from Emory University. She has taught at several American universities and is currently a senior lecturer at the Università degli Studi di Bologna, Italy. In addition to a forthcoming book on anthropology for a general audience, she is the author of *Measuring Mamma's Milk: Fascism and the Medicalization of Maternity in Italy* (Ann Arbor: University of Michigan Press, 2000).

ABOUT MACAT

GREAT WORKS FOR CRITICAL THINKING

Macat is focused on making the ideas of the world's great thinkers accessible and comprehensible to everybody, everywhere, in ways that promote the development of enhanced critical thinking skills.

It works with leading academics from the world's top universities to produce new analyses that focus on the ideas and the impact of the most influential works ever written across a wide variety of academic disciplines. Each of the works that sit at the heart of its growing library is an enduring example of great thinking. But by setting them in context – and looking at the influences that shaped their authors, as well as the responses they provoked – Macat encourages readers to look at these classics and game-changers with fresh eyes. Readers learn to think, engage and challenge their ideas, rather than simply accepting them.

'Macat offers an amazing first-of-its-kind tool for interdisciplinary learning and research. Its focus on works that transformed their disciplines and its rigorous approach, drawing on the world's leading experts and educational institutions, opens up a world-class education to anyone.'

Andreas Schleicher,
Director for Education and Skills, Organisation for Economic
Co-operation and Development

'Macat is taking on some of the major challenges in university education … They have drawn together a strong team of active academics who are producing teaching materials that are novel in the breadth of their approach.'

Prof Lord Broers,
former Vice-Chancellor of the University of Cambridge

'The Macat vision is exceptionally exciting. It focuses upon new modes of learning which analyse and explain seminal texts which have profoundly influenced world thinking and so social and economic development. It promotes the kind of critical thinking which is essential for any society and economy. This is the learning of the future.'

Rt Hon Charles Clarke, former UK Secretary of State for Education

'The Macat analyses provide immediate access to the critical conversation surrounding the books that have shaped their respective discipline, which will make them an invaluable resource to all of those, students and teachers, working in the field.'

Professor William Tronzo, University of California at San Diego

WAYS IN TO THE TEXT

KEY POINTS

- Betty Friedan was a notably influential American journalist and feminist* activist who lived from 1921 to 2006.

- *The Feminine Mystique* spelled out the reasons for widespread physical, emotional, and mental disturbances among American housewives in the 15 years following World War II.*

- The best-selling book tackled the nameless misery many women were suffering and provided answers—helping to revive the dormant feminist movement and contributing to the massive social changes of the 1970s.

Who Was Betty Friedan?

Betty Friedan, the author of *The Feminine Mystique* (1963), was born Bettye Naomi Goldstein in 1921 in the US state of Illinois to Jewish parents of Russian and Hungarian heritage. Her mother Miriam was a writer and her father, Harry, was a jeweler with his own store. Friedan was a bright, headstrong child who began writing about politics in high school. She edited her college's newspaper during the early years of World War II, when it focused on the labor movement* in America and fascism* in Europe; the "labor movement" refers to the organizations known as unions formed by workers with the aim of bettering things such as pay and working conditions; "fascism" is an extreme right-wing political ideology centered on notions of nationhood, state control, and the suppression of dissent.

Friedan studied psychology at Smith College*—a women's college—and graduated summa cum laude (with highest honors) in 1942. She won a graduate fellowship that took her to the University of California at Berkeley.* She was offered a second fellowship but decided against pursing a doctoral degree and moved to New York to become a political activist and journalist. Four years later she married Carl Friedan, moved to the suburbs, and had three children.

Friedan was fired from her job as a journalist for being pregnant but continued writing as a freelancer by moving into women's magazines. In 1957 she sent a questionnaire to her college classmates, asking how they had fared in the 15 years since graduation. Their responses were a revelation and prompted Friedan to write *The Feminine Mystique,* the 1963 study of a widespread, unnamed distress among America's housewives. The book helped to reignite the women's movement that went on to achieve huge changes in the social and legal status of women. Friedan died on her 85th birthday in 2006.

What Does *The Feminine Mystique* Say?

Freidan's landmark text exposes and explains why persuading middle-class American women to retreat to the home after World War II left them in such a state of unease. The "feminine mystique" identified in the work describes the idea that a woman's complete devotion to house, husband, and children was of equal value to a man's role as breadwinner,* replacing earlier ideas of men's natural superiority and women's inferiority with an illusion of equality based on absolute difference. According to this illusion, women and men were equals legally and intellectually but simply wanted different things out of life; and, accordingly, women were encouraged not to compete with men in education and the workplace so as to protect their feminine personality from the supposed "masculinization" that women underwent when pursuing greater opportunities in the first half of the twentieth century. The mystique really took hold in the 1950s, when members of Friedan's generation were told that the happy and well-groomed housewife was the truest expression of femininity.

This thinking also worked to make women blame themselves for their own distress. Rather than being trapped in a life that made them anxious and wasted their talents, they were failing to adjust properly to their natural role as wives and mothers.

In *The Feminine Mystique*, however, Friedan shows that the distress this caused was the predictable result of repetitive work and thwarted potential, which affects all people regardless of their sex,* and that the feminine mystique is counterproductive to its own goals. It does not create the best possible marital relationships and parenting, or make the home a safe refuge from a chaotic world. It even results in more difficulty with childbirth and can harm reproductive health.

Friedan gave a name to this form of suffering that women blamed on themselves. Isolated in their homemaking lives and told that the key to their existence was living for and through others, women sought help from doctors and psychologists. These authority figures treated their problems as a failure of femininity. What is more, the mystique did not have a plan for older women. Sooner or later, time deprived them of the possibility of another baby to affirm their existence. As a result, women's physical and mental-health problems worsened with age.

Friedan's book makes a powerful argument for seeing both women and men as people above all else. The women's movement of the 1960s, 1970s, and 1980s, which sought to dismantle the legal and social framework that restricted women's economic, social, and reproductive independence, shared this vision. The book played a key role in awakening the country to the need of doing away with the feminine mystique and unleashing the human potential it wasted.

The Feminine Mystique sold three million copies in the first three years and has been translated and distributed throughout the world. Friedan added an epilogue in 1974 and another chapter in 1997. It is still considered one of the most important books of the twentieth century, both by supporters and by conservatives who blame it for causing women's discontent and undesirable social changes.

Why Does *The Feminine Mystique* Matter?

Friedan's ideas lit a fuse in 1963, helping to explode the stifling assumptions about the role of women and men that were causing tensions and unease in countless American homes. Her book managed to inspire women and help awaken the feminist movement, while at the same time provoking a storm of derision from powerful areas of society.

She showed readers that they were not alone in needing more than to live through housework, husbands, and children. The housewife of the years following World War II was not programmed by nature but created by society. Friedan showed that advertisers and their clients had a financial stake in the mystique because it was a powerful tool in selling products. She outlined the historical circumstances that made the belief system psychologically compelling and economically feasible. Most importantly, she pointed to a way out. She argued that women must shake off the mystique and take up the meaningful training or work of which they were capable.

The book is important for its place in the history of women's and social movements in the United States. Friedan wrote for a general audience in a clear and compelling style. Her ideas had a broad impact, inspiring women and men to resist the feminine mystique and fight for changes to laws and customs that penalized women.

More than five decades on, the debate around male and female roles and responsibilities for cooking, cleaning, and childcare is far from over. In many parts of the world in the twenty-first century, women are still deemed to belong in the home while men go out to work. Or women are expected to carry the full burden of household duties while also working. So the forces explored by Friedan remain relevant. Cultural beliefs about inborn differences between sexes, ethnic groups, and social classes still limit people's opportunities and economic situations. Friedan shows the importance of a critical approach to expert pronouncements about "human nature" in any era.

Finally, the core concept of self-actualization* (the development and continued exercise of individual abilities) through sustained effort at school and work is relevant to personal life. Friedan shows that people with a solid sense of self and purpose in the community enjoy better health and relationships. They are better equipped to handle the demands of housework and childrearing, as well—the final word against the feminine mystique.

SECTION 1
INFLUENCES

THE AUTHOR AND THE HISTORICAL CONTEXT

KEY POINTS

- Betty Friedan's *The Feminine Mystique* struck a deep chord among women and men in 1963 and remains relevant today as gender* inequalities continue to affect women and men.

- Friedan wrote the book having lived as a housewife while working for magazines that painted a glowing picture of domesticated women, and having asked her college classmates how they were faring 15 years after graduation.

- She wrote at a time when postwar psychological desolation, economic prosperity, and suburban development led many middle-class couples to retreat to domestic life.

Why Read this Text?

Betty Friedan's *The Feminine Mystique* provoked intense reactions from the moment it appeared in 1963, ranging from great admiration to intense disapproval. The book immediately struck a chord with women who shared the same isolating sense of being trapped. Their lives left them frustrated, with a loss of personal identity and a tendency to blame themselves for their own anguish. Friedan identified an unnamed problem affecting women, men, and children with allegedly "perfect" lives (identified by the term "the feminine mystique"), traced its sources, and suggested a way out.

The book has been credited with launching the mid-twentieth-century Second Wave* feminist* movement (following the First

> **❝** After I finished each chapter, a part of me would wonder, Am I crazy? But there was also a growing feeling of calm, strong, gut-sureness as the clues fitted together, which must be the same kind of feeling a scientist has ... Only this was not just abstract and conceptual ... If women were really *people* ... then all the things that kept them from being full people in our society would have to be changed. And women ... would see their place on a false pedestal, even their glorification as sexual objects, for the putdown it was. **❞**
>
> Betty Friedan, *The Feminine Mystique*

Wave* of the nineteenth century) and starting a social revolution;[1] it has even been called a book that "pulled the trigger on history."[2] Friedan's influence is plain to see in literary portrayals of housewife existence such as the Canadian novelist Margaret Atwood's* *The Handmaid's Tale* (1986) and the American author Michael Cunningham's* *The Hours* (1998).[3] The US Department of Labor includes the book among the top 10 "Books That Shaped Work in America."[4] In 2006, a committee at New York University* ranked it 37th among the best works of twentieth-century journalism. At the other extreme, in 2007 the conservative magazine *Human Events* placed it seventh among the 10 "most harmful books of the nineteenth and twentieth centuries," in company with the deeply racist *Mein Kampf* ("My Struggle") of Adolf Hitler,* the dictator who led Germany during World War II.[5] The American right-wing commentator Kate O'Beirne's* 2005 book includes Friedan among *Women Who Made the World Worse.*[6]

The book's key role in the struggle for gender equality in the 1970s and beyond has led to many urban myths* about it and misinterpretations of its message. Understanding its true content is one reason why the book should be read today. Another is that the subject of its criticism, which Friedan designates by the term "the feminine mystique," has not disappeared from contemporary society. Friedan's analysis remains useful for understanding the persistence and consequences of failing to see women as "no more, no less" than human beings.[7]

Author's Life

Betty Friedan was born Bettye Naomi Goldstein in Peoria, a city in the US state of Illinois, in 1921. Her father was an immigrant from Russia and her mother was second-generation Hungarian American. Friedan's mother worked as writer and editor of the women's section of the local newspaper until her marriage, returning years later when her husband fell ill.[8]

As a child, Friedan was difficult and temperamental. Her parents consulted a psychologist. He told them to "leave the brilliant girl to her own devices."[9]

Friedan graduated summa cum laude (with highest honors) with a degree in psychology from Smith College* in 1942. She spent the following year at the University of California at Berkeley* on a fellowship. Friedan explained her decision not to take a second fellowship as the result of pressure from a boyfriend, but her move to New York to work as an activist journalist while the country was at war suggests more political motivations.[10]

In 1947, Friedan married Carl Friedan, a theater producer who became an advertising executive. She continued to write while raising their three children in suburbs close to New York City. She also lectured at New York University* and the private university called the New School.* In 1957, Friedan sent questionnaires to 200 of her college classmates, asking about their lives and how they felt about them. The responses, along with additional interviews and research, were the basis for *The Feminine Mystique*.

Following publication, Friedan called for gender equality and social change, especially in the workplace, government, reproductive rights, and childcare. She wrote several more books and continued to teach at universities including New York University, the New School, Yale University,* and the University of Southern California.* She cofounded the National Organization for Women (NOW)* in 1966 and served as its president until 1970. She and her family moved to the city, in part to escape the exclusion they suffered because of *The Feminine Mystique*.[11] Friedan and her husband divorced in 1969. In 1970, Friedan led the Women's Strike for Equality* march in New York to commemorate 50 years of women's suffrage* (the right to vote). She died of heart failure on her 85th birthday in February 2006 at her home in Washington, DC.

Author's Background

Betty Friedan wrote about American society in the mid-twentieth century from the point of view of an educated woman who had grown up in a Jewish family during the catastrophic economic downturn of the 1920s and 1930s known as the Great Depression,* the political turmoil of the interwar period, and the beginnings of World War II.* She began to write critically about national and world events in high school. Her education and political activism informed her analysis of middle-class women's social role and personal struggles in *The Feminine Mystique*.

At Smith College,* Friedan edited the college newspaper when it was a forum for criticism of European fascism* (an oppressive form of extreme right-wing ideology instituted in Italy and Germany) and advocacy for workers' rights at home, including unionization of the college cleaning staff (a union is an organization founded by workers of a particular industry with the aim of securing things such as increased pay or better working conditions). After college, she wrote for left-wing publications in New York and was involved in Popular Front* union activism; the Popular Front was a coalition of left-wing political parties formed in Europe and the United States during the 1930s to oppose fascism and promote social reform without requiring the destruction of capitalism. Friedan fought against racism, sexism, and corporate power and wrote about women's wartime employment and the efforts of unions to end unequal pay and opportunities for women workers.[12]

From 1943 to 1946, Friedan wrote for the nation's leading leftist news service, the Federated Press. From 1946 to 1952 she wrote for *UE News*, the publication of the United Electrical, Radio, and Machine Workers union. She was fired during her second pregnancy instead of receiving maternity leave and moved on to write freelance articles for women's magazines including *Good Housekeeping*, *Ladies' Home Journal*, and *Redbook*.[13]

Friedan's political savvy, her education in psychology, and her role in the media's presentation of middle-class gender roles gave her a unique perspective on the dramatic postwar trend toward early marriage and large families. Firsthand experience of suburban life gave her the tools for focused observation and interviewing. Friedan's ability as a writer meant she could bring all these elements together in a book that is both complex and accessible.

NOTES

1   Gail Collins, "Introduction," in *The Feminine Mystique*, by Betty Friedan (New York: W. W. Norton & Company, 2013), xi.

2   Alvin Toffler, cover of *The Feminine Mystique*, by Betty Friedan (New York: W. W. Norton & Company, 2001).

3   Margaret Atwood, *The Handmaid's Tale* (Boston, MA: Houghton Mifflin, 1986); Michael Cunningham, The Hours (New York: Farrar, Strauss, and Giroux, 1998).

4   "Books That Shaped Work in America," United States Department of Labor, accessed December 23, 2015, http://www.dol.gov/100/books-shaped-work/initiative.htm.

5   Stephanie Coontz, *A Strange Stirring:* The Feminine Mystique and *American Women at the Dawn of the 1960s* (New York: Basic Books, 2011), xv–xvi.

6   Kate O'Beirne, *Women Who Made the World Worse: And How Their Radical Feminist Assault Is Ruining Our Schools, Families, Military, and Sports* (New York: Sentinel, 2005).

7   Betty Friedan, *The Feminine Mystique* (New York: W. W. Norton & Company, 2013), 516.

8   Susan Oliver, *Betty Friedan: The Personal Is Political* (New York: Pearson Longman, 2008), 4–5.

9   Oliver, Betty Friedan, 9.

10 Daniel Horowitz, *Betty Friedan and the Making of The Feminine Mystique: The American Left, the Cold War, and Modern Feminism* (Amherst, MA: University of Massachusetts Press, 1998).

11 Friedan, *The Feminine Mystique*, 459

12 Horowitz, *Betty Friedan*, xi.

13 Horowitz, *Betty Friedan*, xi.

ACADEMIC CONTEXT

KEY POINTS

- *The Feminine Mystique* tackles how women and men's roles—the behavior expected of them and their status in society and law—are decided according to cultural beliefs about sex differences.

- Betty Friedan was writing at a time when several academic disciplines in the United States agreed (despite evidence to the contrary) that women's sexual and reproductive role defined their thinking and social position.

- She shows how theories from anthropology* and sociology,* along with the ideas of Sigmund Freud*—the founder of the therapeutic and theoretical approach to the unconscious mind known as psychoanalysis*—were used selectively to support the supposed naturalness of middle-class views of femininity.

The Work In Its Context

Betty Friedan's *The Feminine Mystique* focuses on the ideal of family in the years following World War II*—the simple (nuclear) family* with clear-cut roles for women and men. Friedan was writing amid great enthusiasm for the ideas about the primary place of sex and sexual frustrations in human psychology developed by Sigmund Freud, the founder of psychoanalysis. She explains that Freud's ideas took hold in the US in the 1940s,[1] when they were used to interpret problems allegedly caused by earlier feminists'* achievements and their impact on boys and men.[2]

For Friedan, Freud's theories were not universal human truths, but the thinking of a particular individual living in a specific era (Europe

> ❝ Instead of destroying old prejudices that restricted women's lives, social science in America merely gave them new authority. By a curious circular process, the insights of psychology and anthropology and sociology, which should have been powerful weapons to free women, somehow canceled each other out, trapping women in dead center. ❞
>
> Betty Friedan, *The Feminine Mystique*

of the late nineteenth and early twentieth century). Freud was himself sexually repressed and fascinated with behavior he and the society of his time and place considered degrading, which led him to see "hysteria" in his female patients in terms of sexual repression. Both his theory about men's sexual jealousy toward their fathers (the "Oedipus complex") and his beliefs about gender were highly personal, she argues.[3] Friedan explains that Freud considered women a "strange, inferior, less-than-human species."[4] Backed by his society as well as Jewish religion, he felt "it was woman's nature to be ruled by man, and her sickness to envy him."[5]

As with his other theories that point toward states of mind and development associated with human anatomy—the "oral" and "anal" stages of growth and sexual development, for example, concerning the pleasure an infant takes in certain sensual experiences at specific points in its development as a social and sexual being—Freud puts women's inferiority down to the lack of a penis. Boys' realization of what it is that distinguishes them from girls results, later, in fear of castration by females bent on the hopeless pursuit of owning the masculine sex organ, which they can only satisfy by having a son.

Freud disdains competitiveness in women, considering it the result of improper upbringing and something that prevents them from realizing their mothering skills. Friedan argues that by writing off professional ambition as repressed penis envy, Freud reveals his attitude toward what he considers a degraded category of humans, unfit for competition, and biologically unable to reach full social and intellectual development.[6]

Overview of the Field

Since scientific evidence disproved the contention that women were less intelligent than men, Freud's followers in the United States focused on women being anatomically unequal to men. Friedan shows how experts sought to protect women against a "neurotic" refusal to accept their destiny, to not resent being excluded from achievement, and to deal appropriately with their penis envy. They taught that rather than harm themselves through work, education, or feminist protest, women should seek fulfillment by becoming wives and mothers.[7]

The psychoanalyst Marynia Farnham* and the journalist and social critic Ferdinand Lundberg* warned that education and careers harmed home life and children and interfered with the achievement of sexual gratification. Good sex depended on women's ability to embrace their natural dependence and passivity.[8] Meanwhile, the psychoanalyst Helene Deutsch* said girls and women did not have to wholly suppress their ambition. It could be channeled toward their fathers' and husbands' lives instead.[9] To achieve normal femininity women had only to give up the "masculinity complex" of personal goals rooted in the presumption of equality.[10]

These beliefs reduced a social problem related to political, legal, and economic inequalities, and the fact of women's isolation in suburban houses, to individual failure to adjust properly to the supposed "realities" of women's sexual roles. By definition, education, careers, and equal rights were harmful to women. Friedan notes that while the mass retreat from a harsh, chaotic world into domestic life had the potentially positive effect of putting sex in a more positive light and allowing women and men to focus on themselves, it also "cast suspicions on the high aspirations of the mind and spirit."[11]

Through the 1940s and 1950s Freud's ideas held sway in the media, educational system, mental health profession, and popular mental health campaigns for parents, children, pregnant women, and the general public. For American women this "Freudian superego worked ... as Freud said the superego works—to perpetuate the past."[12]

Academic Influences

Friedan studied psychology during the heyday of Freudian psychoanalysis in the United States. The developmental psychologist* and psychoanalyst Erik Erikson,* who had been trained by Anna Freud (Sigmund Freud's youngest daughter), was on the faculty at Berkeley* the year Friedan studied at that university. Friedan also came across the functionalist* tradition popular in sociology and anthropology through the first half of the twentieth century (sociology is the study of the history and functioning of human society and the nature of social behavior; anthropology is the study of humankind, commonly taking the form of research into cultural and social behavior and history).

According to the functionalist approach to anthropology and sociology, social institutions work together much like parts of the human body. They keep everything together and stable without duplicating any task. In terms of gender roles, the influential sociologist Talcott Parsons* argued, "Absolute equality of opportunity is clearly incompatible with any positive solidarity of the family."[13] While he recognized the potential harm of seeing women's reproductive function as complementary to men's function as the breadwinner,* Parsons said there was no choice and women must simply adjust. The sociologist Mirra Komarovsky* also said girls had to learn and adapt to their sex-determined gender role—which she accepted was given by society not nature—by withdrawing from competition at school or work and suppressing unfeminine interests or talents. Women's identity should come from their gender role, not a profession.[14]

Anthropology could have counteracted Freudian-functional views of gender following the research of the anthropologist Margaret Mead* in New Guinea, which led her to conclude that female and male personality traits are no more determined by biology than the clothing or manners assigned to each gender.[15] But this idea did not play nearly as well as her argument that men's roles are granted by society and the role of the woman is decided by nature. This was based on her observation that Samoan and other Pacific Island men envy and venerate pregnant women.[16] Friedan points out that even though Western societies glorify men's creative and intellectual pursuits—not women's reproductive functions—Mead's ideas were taken as proof that career and motherhood are mutually exclusive.[17]

NOTES

1   Betty Friedan, *The Feminine Mystique* (New York: W. W. Norton & Company, 2013), 110.

2   See Emily Martin, *The Woman in the Body: A Cultural Analysis of Reproduction* (Boston, MA: Beacon Press, 1987).

3   Friedan, *The Feminine Mystique*, 120.

4   Friedan, *The Feminine Mystique*, 116.

5   Friedan, *The Feminine Mystique*, 117.

6   Friedan, *The Feminine Mystique*, 125–6.

7   Friedan, *The Feminine Mystique*, 130.

8   Friedan, *The Feminine Mystique*, 131; *Marynia Farnham and Ferdinand Lundberg, Modern Woman: The Lost Sex* (New York: Harper & Brothers, 1947).

9   Helene Deutsch, *The Psychology of Women: A Psychoanalytic Interpretation* (Allyn & Bacon, 1943, 1945).

10 Friedan, *The Feminine Mystique*, 133.

11 Friedan, *The Feminine Mystique*, 136.

12 Friedan, *The Feminine Mystique*, 137.

13 Friedan, *The Feminine Mystique*, 147.

14 Friedan, *The Feminine Mystique*, 147–9; Mirra Komarovsky, *Women in the Modern World: Their Education and Their Dilemmas* (Boston, MA: Little, Brown & Co., 1953); Talcott Parsons, *Essays in Sociological Theory* (New York: Free Press, 1958).

15 Friedan, *The Feminine Mystique*, 156; Margaret Mead, *Sex and Temperament in Three Primitive Societies* (New York: William Morrow, 1935).

16 Friedan, *The Feminine Mystique*, 153; Margaret Mead, *Male and Female: A Study of the Sexes in a Changing World* (New York: William Morrow, 1949).

17 Friedan, *The Feminine Mystique*, 161; see also Friedan, *The Feminine Mystique*, 167, 210.

MODULE 3
THE PROBLEM

KEY POINTS

- Betty Friedan set out to identify why widespread distress among middle-class American women accompanied the increase in the number of housewives and a rocketing birthrate following World War II.*

- Women's emotional distress was blamed on education and paid work being at odds with femininity and their role in the home, where they needed to embrace their position as housewife.

- *The Feminine Mystique* revealed historical reasons for the rise in housewifery and showed how this created an idealized vision of women that caused serious problems for women, men, families, and society.

Core Question

In *The Feminine Mystique*, Betty Friedan asks why the distress of housewives in the United States following World War II met with insistence from all sides that "their role was to seek fulfillment as wives and mothers."[1]

Friedan identified what she termed "the problem that has no name" as the loss of identity and sense of worthlessness women suffer in a role that dictates complete economic and emotional dependence on a husband and living through the achievements only of her man and her children. She also identified the key tool used by society to push women into accepting this role: the vision of femininity as selfless, joyful devotion to husband, children, and housework; this—what she termed the feminine mystique—was the product of a woman's precious, natural, and mysterious capacity to create life.

> 66 Imaginatively she is of the highest importance; practically she is completely insignificant ... Some of the most inspired words, some of the most profound thoughts in literature fall from her lips; in real life she could hardly read, scarcely spell, and was the property of her husband. 99
>
> Virginia Woolf, *A Room of One's Own*

Friedan notes that before the 1950s the lives of girls and women improved thanks to the achievements of nineteenth- and early twentieth-century feminists* (now known as First Wave* feminists) who had campaigned for equality in matters regarding property, education, wages, and voting rights. By 1920, women made up 47 percent of college students.[2] Educated, professional American women astounded European visitors with their capability and independence.

Housework did not change for the better during the first decades of the twentieth century, though, especially with more people moving from farms to cities. Pioneer and farmwomen had worked in a joint enterprise with their husbands, with a clear productive role. For urban women, housework was time-consuming, physically demanding drudgery without laborsaving devices or refrigerated, prepackaged food. Working-class women had factory and service jobs in addition to housework. Continued gender* discrimination kept three-quarters of women from working outside the home in spite of their education, leaving housewives of the 1930s and 1940s frustrated and embittered.[3] Friedan explains that, under the spell of the feminine mystique, many a daughter set out to do better at fulfilling herself in that same role, and "never read the lesson of her mother's life."[4]

The Participants
Friedan explains that after a period of intense public engagement

during World War II, women retreated in great numbers from education and work outside the home. The proportion of workers was down to one-third of American women by the late 1950s. While the proportion of female industrial workers rose steadily after the war, women in professions requiring education and personal commitment declined. Of the top students in high school, girls were more than twice as likely as boys not to attend college. By 1958, the proportion of college students in the United States who were female dropped to 35 percent. In the mid-1950s, girls were far more likely than boys to quit college before graduating. Girls were more prone to drop out to get married or through fear of becoming unmarriageable than as a result of academic failure.[5]

The booming postwar economy created a huge middle class with a higher standard of living than ever before. Ownership of houses, cars, and televisions skyrocketed. Although men displaced women from jobs and excluded them from the better positions, women did not retreat to the home for lack of opportunities. There were shortages even in fields such as teaching, nursing, and clerical work. Instead, women diverted their energy into housework that was more time-consuming in spite of laborsaving appliances and the availability of manufactured goods previously made in the home.[6]

By the late 1950s the average age for a woman to get married was 20 and falling, the youngest in the country's history and among industrialized nations. The birthrate rose to levels approaching those of developing nations in Asia and Africa. Friedan notes that this was odd compared to Europe and Japan, where there was a blip after the war but no sustained increase in childbearing. Furthermore, educated women led the race to large families.[7]

The explanation lies in what Friedan terms the feminine mystique, which redefined the role of housewife as a noble calling on a par with men's work. Women were forced to choose between its vision of femininity and independent personhood.

The Contemporary Debate

Friedan explains that men and women alike came through World War II feeling vulnerable, frightened, and homesick. Soldiers yearned for childhood and home, especially maternal care. Friedan outlines how the postwar economic boom allowed all that "pent-up hunger for marriage, home, and children" to be satisfied and "the whole nation stopped growing up."[8] This urge to turn inward against a chaotic world was fed by illusions about idealized family relationships. Scholars, mental health workers, advertisers, and artists focused on individual problems in sex and love rather than "probing too deeply for the common causes of man's suffering."[9]

According to the theories of Sigmund Freud,* the founder of the theoretical and therapeutic approach to the mind known as psychoanalysis,* work was detrimental to the sexual and reproductive functions of women; indeed, they pointed the finger at mothers for every possible problem in their children. In the 1940s, the deep troubles of soldiers and veterans were blamed on the current generation of empowered women, even though these men's own mothers were from previous generations. By the 1950s this flawed logic was used to convince women once again to subjugate their identities to those of their husbands and children.[10] The childcare centers created by the government for working women closed down.[11]

In 1948, the human biologist Alfred Kinsey* produced the first of his two influential "reports" on sexuality. In it, he claimed (incorrectly) that educated women were especially unable to experience orgasm, fueling the belief that intellectual activity interfered with sexual fulfillment.[12] Abandoned babies were assumed (also incorrectly) to have been left by working mothers. Studies claiming to link juvenile delinquency to women working received far more attention than research showing the positive effects of women's work on mothers and their children. Together these mistaken ideas about biological sex propped up the false choice between femininity and individuality identified by Friedan.[13]

NOTES

1 Betty Friedan, *The Feminine Mystique* (New York: W. W. Norton & Company, 2013), 1.

2 Friedan, *The Feminine Mystique*, 2.

3 Friedan, *The Feminine Mystique*, 222.

4 Friedan, *The Feminine Mystique*, 71.

5 Friedan, *The Feminine Mystique*, 2, 172, 187, 217.

6 Friedan, *The Feminine Mystique*, 217.

7 Friedan, *The Feminine Mystique*, 2, 187, 214.

8 Friedan, *The Feminine Mystique*, 213, 217.

9 Friedan, *The Feminine Mystique*, 219.

10 Friedan, *The Feminine Mystique*, 221–5.

11 Friedan, *The Feminine Mystique*, 216.

12 Alfred Charles Kinsey et al., *Sexual Behavior in the Human Male* (Bloomington: Indiana University Press, 1949); Alfred Charles Kinsey et al., *Sexual Behavior in the Human Female* (Bloomington: Indiana University Press, 1953).

13 Betty Friedan, *The Feminine Mystique*, 226–9.

MODULE 4
THE AUTHOR'S CONTRIBUTION

KEY POINTS

- Powerful forces in the United States following World War II* encouraged women to retreat into homemaking by promoting the illusion that femininity meant giving up identity and growth along with educational and professional attainment.

- In *The Feminine Mystique*, Betty Friedan showed that 1950s gender* roles and expectations were convenient ways to manipulate women, and she cast doubt on widespread assumptions about differences between the sexes.

- Friedan's concept of the feminine mystique united insights from sociology,* feminist* theory, history, and marketing, in the face of prevailing academic, professional, and popular beliefs about gender.

Author's Aims

Betty Friedan identified deep psychological and physical suffering in the housewives of her generation, between the years 1945 and 1960. In *The Feminine Mystique* she sets out to explain why so many women were so miserable in postwar America.

As her 15th reunion at Smith College* approached in 1957, Friedan decided to find out what had become of her female classmates since their graduation. She sent out 200 questionnaires and the responses from those women became the basis for *The Feminine Mystique*. In 1959, Friedan spent a week with fourth-year students at Smith, then interviewed students and housewives around the country. She also analyzed scholarly and popular literature of the time, including

> **❝** Redbook commented: 'Few women would want to thumb their noses at husbands, children and community and go off on their own. Those who do may be talented individuals, but they rarely are successful women.' **❞**
>
> Betty Friedan, *The Feminine Mystique*

advertisements and the women's magazines she knew as a freelance writer.

When World War II ended, American women received the same message from all sides. The essence of femininity was giving up all personal ambition and devoting themselves to the family. Work that helped with family expenses or occupied them until marriage was acceptable so long as it did not threaten the status of men as breadwinners* or take the prestigious jobs reserved for them. Women were told that their sexuality* and motherliness ruled out competitiveness, strength, and intellectual achievement. It was noble and gratifying to leave all decision-making and striving in the world to men. Women were told that housework was no longer drudgery. It was a technical and scientific career requiring specialized products and training through books and magazines devoted to parenting and how to advance the husband's career and please him sexually.[1]

In reality, housework was among the most unskilled and exploitative jobs. Women proved they were equally capable at school and work, and farm and factory women were hardly physically weak and passive.[2] Even the marketers knew that women were competitive. A 1962 advertisement in the *New York Times* for sexy clothing for little girls, for instance, said, "She Too Can Join the Man-Trap Set."[3] The task for Friedan was to explain how American culture closed this gap between the reality and the mystique.

Approach

Women's magazines were a powerful force in the definition of femininity as it applied to the housewife. Friedan explains that in the 1930s and 1940s, the heroines in short fiction were spirited, determined, independent women who flew airplanes, became scientists, took challenging jobs, and still found love. "The ideal of yesterday's housewives," these characters were admired, not despised, by men.[4] Their stories were written by women.

That all changed in the 1950s. Men wrote the love stories and made them about housewives. Working women only featured to be congratulated on giving up the top positions to men, using their earnings for the family, and "looking and acting far more feminine than the 'emancipated' girl" of the 1920s and 1930s.[5] Magazines contrasted the placid housewife with domineering, sexually unappealing professional women or overzealous volunteers as a lesson against ambition, activity, and envy.

Women writers and editors contributed amusing pieces about family life as if they were housewives.[6] Serious fiction gave way to the "service" article—extended advertisements. Articles about world events, art, and science were replaced with stories about victims of sickness and physical disabilities. The rest was devoted to beauty, babies and parenting, home decoration, and celebrities. Complex, serious female actors of the 1940s, such as Marlene Dietrich* and Greta Garbo,* were replaced by women representing sensuality or youthful motherliness such as Marilyn Monroe* and Debbie Reynolds.* Overall, the magazines treated their readers as superficial, emotional children uninterested in serious topics. Even the font size was increased.[7]

Women accounted for three-quarters of consumer spending, so marketers taunted them with images of graceful, up-to-date housekeeping and eternal youthfulness in the company of husbands and small children.[8] They knew that "women will buy more things if they are kept in the underused, nameless-yearning, energy-to-get-rid-of state of being housewives."[9] Marketers presented shopping as the path to creative expression, self-realization, and social status. The trick was to present getting a bargain as a concrete achievement and substitute for earnings.[10]

Contribution in Context

Friedan's analysis is built on a critique of contemporary scholars. She acknowledges the developmental psychologist* and psychoanalyst* Erik Erikson* for his ideas on identity formation, although she emphasizes that she uses them in a novel way by considering girls and women. However, she does not mention the social critics and First Wave* feminists of the nineteenth and early twentieth centuries who had identified the same gender beliefs and harmful consequences described in *The Feminine Mystique*.

The social theorist Charlotte Perkins Gilman's* 1892 essay "The Yellow Wall-Paper" describes the same progressive psychological and physical effects of enforced domesticity and exclusion from "congenial work, with excitement and change," that Friedan outlines.[11] The South African author Olive Schreiner's* 1911 book *Women and Labor* argues that domestic confinement combined with laborsaving devices results in a parasitical role for women.[12] In the 1920s, the British author Virginia Woolf's* novels and lectures explore the subjective experience of women in a male-dominated society.[13]

The Russian American sociologist Mirra Komarovsky's* *Women in the Modern World* (1953) analyzes the importance of education and work for women. Friedan criticizes Komarovsky's endorsement of accommodation to gender roles that she knew to be culturally constructed rather than "natural."[14] The influential French social theorist Simone de Beauvoir's *The Second Sex*, published in English the same year, argues that the restriction of women to a domestic role distorts marital relationships and women's personality through their dependence on men for an identity.[15] Friedan merely notes that de Beauvoir's work was dismissed in the United States as relevant only to France.[16]

A 1956 book by the sociologists Alva Myrdal* and Viola Klein* exposed the glorification of women's domestic role as a disguise for contempt and a means of silencing women while failing to address inequality.[17] Critical essays on glorified homemaking appeared in elite American magazines such as *Harper's*, the *Atlantic Monthly*, and the *Nation*.[18] Marketers' conscious manipulation of women's desires and spending was discussed by the American social critic Vance Packard* in 1957 in *The Hidden Persuaders*.[19]

NOTES

1 Betty Friedan, *The Feminine Mystique* (New York: W. W. Norton & Company, 2013), 216–17.

2 Friedan, *The Feminine Mystique*, 101, 253.

3 Friedan, *The Feminine Mystique*, 3. Regarding women's competitiveness and advertising, see also 451.

4 Friedan, *The Feminine Mystique*, 31.

5 Friedan, *The Feminine Mystique*, 54–5.

6 Friedan, *The Feminine Mystique*, 51–2.

7 Friedan, *The Feminine Mystique*, 37, 47–8.

8 Friedan, *The Feminine Mystique*, 37, 270–1.

9 Friedan, *The Feminine Mystique*, 243.

10 Friedan, *The Feminine Mystique*, 245, 259, 263–5.

11 Charlotte Perkins Gilman, "The Yellow Wall-Paper," *New England Magazine* 11, no. 5 (1892): 647–56.

12 Olive Schreiner, *Women and Labor* (New York: Frederick A. Stokes, 1911).

13 See Virginia Woolf, *Mrs. Dalloway* (London: Hogarth Press, 1925); *To the Lighthouse* (London: Hogarth Press, 1927); *A Room of One's Own* and *Three Guineas* (Oxford: Oxford University Press, 2015).

14 Friedan, The Feminine Mystique, 149; Stefanie Coontz, *A Strange Stirring: The Feminine Mystique and American Women at the Dawn of the 1960s* (New York: Basic Books, 2011), 66; Mirra Komarovsky, *Women in the Modern World: Their Education and Their Dilemmas* (Boston, MA: Little, Brown & Co., 1953).

15 Simone de Beauvoir, *The Second Sex* (New York: Vintage, 1953). Ten years after the book, Friedan acknowledged Simone de Beauvoir for having identified the psychological effects of the domestic role, but discounted the influence on her own feminist thought. Coontz, *A Strange Stirring*, 43.

16 Friedan, *The Feminine Mystique*, 6. In addition, Friedan mentions de Beauvoir only once in *The Fountain of Age* (New York: Simon & Schuster, 2006), even though the latter had written *The Coming of Age* (New York: Putnam, 1972) on cultural beliefs about aging and gender more than 30 years earlier.

17 Coontz, *A Strange Stirring*, 66; Alva Myrdal and Viola Klein, *Woman's Two Roles: Home and Work* (London: Routledge & Kegan Paul, 1956).

18 Coontz, *A Strange Stirring*, 66.

19 Vance Packard, *The Hidden Persuaders* (Philadelphia: David McKay Company, 1957).

SECTION 2
IDEAS

MAIN IDEAS

KEY POINTS

- *The Feminine Mystique* explores how postwar America reversed the trend for women to have a more equal role in the world in favor of a mindset according to which men went to work and women stayed home to cook, clean, and raise children.

- Betty Friedan argues that the gender beliefs of the United States in the mid-twentieth century pushed women into an all-consuming domesticity that prevented them and their husbands from developing into proper adults, damaging them both.

- She analyzes individual women's experiences in the context of pressures from society and prevailing theories about women's role to address the serious suffering and heavy costs to society in lost human potential.

Key Themes

Betty Friedan's core argument in *The Feminine Mystique* is that an alteration in ideas about conventional femininity in the United States in the years following World War II* pushed women into the home, creating serious problems for them, their families, and society as a whole.

Following World War II, femininity was held up as a mysterious essence that linked women's childbearing function to natural homemaking abilities and inclinations. Unlike previous gender ideologies based on the unsustainable idea of female inferiority dictated by nature or religion, this new mindset claims femininity is not unequal to masculinity—it is simply different.[1] At the same time,

> **❝** The feminine mystique says that the highest value and the only commitment for women is the fulfillment of their own femininity ... this femininity is so mysterious and intuitive and close to the creation and origin of life that man-made science may never be able to understand it ... The mistake, says the mystique, the root of women's troubles in the past is that women envied men, women tried to be like men, instead of accepting their own nature, which can find fulfillment only in sexual passivity, male domination, and nurturing maternal love. **❞**
>
> Betty Friedan, *The Feminine Mystique*

it places women in a position of complete economic and social dependence on men. This is in spite of trends that began in the nineteenth century away from the exclusion of women from higher education, well-paid professions and independent legal status.

Friedan traces the many pressures on women and men to conform to this idea of "the feminine mystique," including media stories and marketing campaigns, academic claims about sex* differences, and changes in educational programs in high schools and universities. There was a great collective nostalgia for the safety of home and family in response to the recent war and the political instability that followed. Rather than continuing the rising trend of female employment, middle-class women turned their energies to increased numbers of children and ever more housework. Housewives in large cities spent the most time on housework (around 80 hours per week), rural women the least (about 60 hours per week), reflecting the effect of new appliances and standards of cleanliness that only multiplied the work.[2] Men and women who had work or other responsibilities outside the home, however, completed housework much faster, and they did not avoid finishing it for fear of being left with no function.[3]

Channeling women into full-time homemaking answered men's desire for a protective, nurturing mother figure. It also cut out competitors in educational institutions and in the workplace. For women, the feminine mystique allowed a retreat from the need to define personal identity and face responsibilities in the wider world that is expected of men. But there was a cost; Friedan shows that work that is out of line with ability and education is frustrating and damaging to anyone, female or male. Furthermore, stunting personal growth has an unhealthy impact on marriages and family relationships.

Exploring the Ideas

As a concerted effort to redefine normality, the feminine mystique pits women against each other. This can be as competitors for and through husbands, or as judges of whether other women are abiding by the gender rules. The mystique isolates women, keeping them from seeing their common plight. It also makes women inflict the same life, with its restricted interests and goals, on their daughters.[4] This stifling of individuality leads to what she termed "the problem that has no name," which worsens with time as children grow up and mothers can no longer look forward to the next baby; she specifically notes an increase in the rates of suicide and hospitalizations for psychiatric disorders in women over 45 and among those whose children had left home.[5]

Women describe emptiness, incompleteness, and nonexistence. They are deprived of privacy, something to look forward to, and the feeling of being alive. They feel physically exhausted but also sleep too much. They report a sense of entrapment, of being shut out from the world, of existing only as their husband's wife and child's mother, not themselves. While constantly in their children's presence and frantically engaged in addressing their every need, mothers feel mentally absent.[6] Housework and their families' demands leave women unable to spend more than 15 minutes on any one thing—hence the popularity of magazines and short fiction.[7] As one woman said of a typical day, "Very little of what I've done has been really necessary or important. Outside pressures lash me through the day."[8]

Friedan found that women blamed themselves and their educations for their frustration. Psychologists emphasized role adjustment, even though they saw that married women patients were more troubled than unmarried ones. They knew that housewives' fatigue, while real, was due not to excessive exertion but to repetitious tasks and a homogenizing role (that is, a role that rendered them all essentially alike).[9]

Friedan shows that the feminine mystique backfired. Far from bringing stability and happiness, it weakened marital relationships and generated widespread alcohol and prescription drug abuse as well as a rise in violence against children.[10] Besides the fatigue, among women there was a rise in ulcers, serious cardiovascular and respiratory problems, and a range of psychological disorders, from mild emotional distress to grave psychotic episodes.*[11] Yet the mystique was accepted so completely that even the deepest despair could not shake it. Friedan recounts the story of a former cancer researcher turned housewife who took her own life the day after taking her children to their doctor's appointments and arranging her daughter's birthday party.[12]

Language and Expression

Friedan put her writing ability and experience as a journalist to work to produce a highly readable, engaging, and organized book. Lengthy quotes from individual women, scholarly texts, and popular magazines and advertisements bring the text to life by vividly illustrating ideas. In some places the writing and arguments are caustic and strident, as in discussions of the inadequacy of volunteer work for women of "intelligence and ability," women's ultimate responsibility for their own choices, and the idea that stunting women's identity is a form of genocide.[13]

Friedan introduced several terms that went on to become household phrases. These include "the problem that has no name" to describe the unacknowledged distress of housewives in the postwar period. The "feminine mystique" refers to the era's anatomy-as-destiny vision of femininity. The psychoanalytic* concept of "masculine protest" is used to describe women who, because of what Sigmund Freud* termed "penis envy,"* compete with or dress as men; Friedan proposes the term "feminine protest" to describe some women's use of exaggerated feminine attitudes and dress to dodge the criticism heaped on earlier feminists.*[14] The American anthropologist* Margaret Mead* and other women in "masculine" professions projected a façade. By looking conventionally feminine they made all women seem more alike than they were.[15] Friedan explains that women adopt the feminine protest to protect themselves, for her quite unnecessarily, from "the dangers inherent in assuming true equality with men."

In hiding behind a "feminine" mask, that is, they do not have to face the challenges that must be met if equality is to be achieved—and by contributing to this damaging, culturally bound vision of women, they ensure that the doors to things such as financial independence and jobs believed to require "masculine" traits remain closed.[16]

NOTES

1   Betty Friedan, *The Feminine Mystique* (New York: W. W. Norton & Company, 2013), 284.

2   For instance, sheets were now to be washed twice a week: Friedan, *The Feminine Mystique*, 287.

3   Friedan, *The Feminine Mystique*, 282–5, 300.

4   Friedan, *The Feminine Mystique*, 279.

5   Friedan, *The Feminine Mystique*, 59, 361–2.

6   Friedan, *The Feminine Mystique*, 355.

7   On the popularity of short fiction in the 1950s and 1960s, see Kurt Vonnegut's autobiographical introduction to his *Bagombo Snuff Box: Uncollected Short Fiction* (New York: G. P. Putnam's Sons, 1999).

8   Friedan, *The Feminine Mystique*, 17.

9   Friedan, *The Feminine Mystique*, 14, 20, 297–9.

10   Friedan, *The Feminine Mystique*, 299–300, 363-4.

11   Friedan, *The Feminine Mystique*, 280, 351.

12   Friedan, *The Feminine Mystique*, 350–1; Friedan (*The Feminine Mystique*, 352) reports that in the 1950s young mothers were by far the majority of adult psychiatric patients.

13   Friedan, *The Feminine Mystique*, 417, 211, 439, respectively.

14   Friedan, *The Feminine Mystique*, 91.

15   See Lise M. Dobrin and Ira Bashkow, "'Arapesh Warfare': Reo Fortune's veiled critique of Margaret Mead's *Sex and Temperament*," *American Anthropologist* 112, no. 3 (2010): 370–83.

16   Friedan, *The Feminine Mystique*, 141, 167.

MODULE 6
SECONDARY IDEAS

KEY POINTS

- *The Feminine Mystique* shows how the ways in which women were educated in preparation for a specifically "feminine" life closes off opportunities for intellectual and personal growth, leading to tensions about roles and responsibilities that extend to sexual problems in marriage and saddle children with excessive motherly attention.

- Betty Friedan argues that being confined in an all-consuming feminine role actually undermines women's ability to meet society's expectations of them as wives, sexual partners, and mothers.

- Contrary to popular opinion at the time, research findings and Friedan's interviews confirm that higher educational levels are associated with improved sexual function.

Other Ideas

In *The Feminine Mystique*, Betty Friedan explains how middle-class gender* roles became more rigid and separate in the 15 years after World War II.*[1] Women learned from an early age that it was more noble to withdraw from higher education and demanding professions, instead creating their identity through a husband and family. Even the new suburban houses, with their open floor plans, expressed the assumption that women did not need a separate existence.[2] Unlike the ardent earlier feminists* who had fought for opportunities and independence, feminine women were expected to placidly shelve their dreams and shun decision-making. But this only served to damage the marital relationship.

Friedan explains that the feminine mystique infantilized women

> ❝ And so the circle tightens. Sex without self, enshrined by the feminine mystique, casts an ever-darkening shadow over man's image of woman and woman's image of herself. It becomes harder and harder for both son and daughter to escape, to find themselves in the world, to love another in human intercourse. ❞
>
> Betty Friedan, *The Feminine Mystique*

in many different ways. They were left to organize parties and play bridge or golf when not occupied with housework.[3] While volunteer work in the new suburbs was needed and meaningful at first, over time it became increasingly superfluous. And top positions such as places on the school board were held by men.[4]

In high school, girls were taught the tasks of their gender role as an academic subject, and in college they were led away from "masculine" fields. Too "flamboyant and abstract," even fine art was to be avoided in favor of ceramics or textiles.[5] Girls disengaged, defending themselves "against the impersonal passions of mind and spirit that college might instill in them—the dangerous non-sexual passions of the intellect."[6] They focused on finding a husband instead of a self, "and each act of self-betrayal tips the scale farther away from identity to passive self-contempt."[7]

Through a self-fulfilling prophecy, educators made women "passive, dependent, conformist, incapable of critical thought or original contribution to society" with the same inevitability as previous eras' denial of education to women.[8] And even though they were aware of the problems caused by the housewife role, they relentlessly continued to push all women into it.[9] This included female professors, who dressed in ultra-feminine clothes, hiding behind what Friedan termed the "feminine protest": a visible way to reject the implications of feminism.

Exploring the Ideas

Restricting women's education was based on the notion, popular in the decades before World War II, that intellectual activity causes low fertility (something derived from the nineteenth-century idea of eugenics,* according to which the human race might be "improved" through, essentially, selective breeding).[10] Friedan shows, to the contrary, that the housewife role undermined marital relationships and interfered with women's sexual fulfillment and reproductive functions. For instance, housewives had more trouble with pregnancy, giving birth, depression following childbirth,* menstruation, and menopause.[11]

Friedan explains that the housewife-breadwinner* set-up allowed men to escape personal growth and often drove couples apart. Men's desire for the unconditional love of a wife-mother extended the parent–child relationship indefinitely.[12] As domestic experts, women jealously guarded their control over children and home. Their complete dependence on men for status and identity rendered them aggressive, dominating, and contemptuous if their husbands failed them. Studies found that wives were the most frustrating things in men's lives, above work or finances.[13]

New sexual problems arose from women's need for sex to affirm their existence and make them feel alive. Women and men had affairs and the rate of separations rocketed.[14] The housewife's pursuit of sexual fulfillment was doomed, however, because it aimed to fill needs that were not sexual—needs for larger goals and purposes in life.[15] Reduced to an object living in a world of objects, she ultimately is "unable to touch in others the individual identity she lacks herself."[16]

The human biologist Alfred Kinsey's* celebrated "Reports" on human sexuality showed a reversal in the 1950s of a decades-long trend in women increasingly experiencing sexual orgasm, and that educated women enjoyed sex more but needed it less than women married before age 20.[17] The psychologist A. H. Maslow* found that "dominant," self-actualized women were more giving of themselves in love and in general than women with a poorly developed ego and low self-esteem.[18] They were less self-centered, more outward-oriented, and surer of themselves and their opinions. They defied popular wisdom through the increased quality of love and sexual satisfaction in their relationships over time. For these women and their partners, there was no hostility, no need for separate roles, no fear of aging. Love was based not on need but more as a gift motivated by "spontaneous admiration."[19]

Overlooked

The feminine mystique rests on the idea that women's work and education compromise their sexual functioning and harm children. Friedan refers to evidence from the United States, as well as countries such as Russia and Israel, that work outside the home does not interfere with women's ability to care for their homes and families.[20] She argues that the housewife role causes mothers to become overly involved in their children's lives, damaging future generations.

Friedan shows how the complete dedication to children prescribed by the feminine mystique leads mothers to enter a state of symbiosis with their offspring—that is, in essence, that their relationship is defined by mutual interdependence and a consequent loss of individual identity; this leads to an inability to discipline them or refuse any demand. Mothers chauffeur their children around and do their homework while making sure they never have to deal with challenges and disappointments. As a result, children lack resourcefulness, motivation, a strong sense of personal identity and goals, and a social conscience. With all their activities organized for them, children spend little time outdoors and grow physically weak.[21]

These traits were seen in children, college students, and soldiers of the late 1950s.[22] They caused concern because boys could not be allowed to go to waste. "The insult, the real reflection on our culture's definition of the role of women, is that as a nation we only noticed something was wrong with women when we saw its effects on their sons."[23]

Beyond spelling out the dangers of overzealous parenting, Friedan suggests that mothers being too close to their children causes virtually every trait she considers undesirable or dangerous in young people. These include teen delinquency (a tendency to antisocial behavior), vandalism, promiscuity, and early sexual activity.[24] Based on the Kinsey Reports' suggestion that in men both early sexual activity and homosexuality are linked to psychological immaturity related to low educational or professional attainment, Friedan includes homosexuality, sexual perversions, fragile ego, the suite of social and mental challenges known as autism, and a preference for same-sex company in her list of undesirable and dangerous traits in young people.[25] This argument is rooted in the same propensity to blame the mother (a propensity derived from the theories of the pioneering psychoanalyst* Sigmund Freud)* that Friedan rails against elsewhere in her book, including previous generations' erroneous assumption that "masculinization" would cause a rise in homosexuality.[26] Moreover, Kinsey's data were unrepresentative and his personal sexual interests heavily influenced his research.[27]

NOTES

1   Friedan uses the terms "sex role" and "sex-directed education," in line with the linguistic conventions of the times.

2   Betty Friedan, *The Feminine Mystique* (New York: W. W. Norton & Company, 2013), 292.

3   Friedan, *The Feminine Mystique*, 412.

4   Friedan, *The Feminine Mystique*, 290, 292.

5   Friedan, *The Feminine Mystique*, 184.

6   Friedan, *The Feminine Mystique*, 177.

7   Friedan, *The Feminine Mystique*, 201. For the effects of gender-role-directed college education, see also *The Feminine Mystique*, 69, 193.

8   Friedan, *The Feminine Mystique*, 207.

9   Friedan, *The Feminine Mystique*, 208.

10 Maria Sophia Quine, *Population Politics in Twentieth-Century Europe: Fascist Dictatorships and Liberal Democracies* (London: Routledge, 1996).

11 Betty Friedan, *The Feminine Mystique*, 318–21. Friedan (*The Feminine Mystique*, 351) reports on a study from Bergen County, New Jersey, in the 1950s that found one in three women suffered postpartum depression or psychotic breakdown, compared to previous estimates of one psychotic breakdown per 400 pregnancies, and one case of less severe depression per 80 pregnancies.

12 Friedan, *The Feminine Mystique*, 363.

13 Friedan, *The Feminine Mystique*, 323–4.

14 Friedan reports that half of all 55-year-old men engaged in extramarital affairs: Friedan, *The Feminine Mystique*, 325, 361. She describes (*The Feminine Mystique*, 311–12) the whole country as swept up in an immature, calculated, vulgar fascination with sex, as seen in art, media, theater, and sex studies.

15 Friedan, *The Feminine Mystique*, 310.

16 Friedan, *The Feminine Mystique*, 316–17.

17 Friedan, *The Feminine Mystique*, 77, 331, 394–5; Alfred Charles Kinsey et al., *Sexual Behavior in the Human Female* (Bloomington: Indiana University Press, 1953).

18 Friedan, *The Feminine Mystique*, 382–91.

19 Friedan, *The Feminine Mystique*, 391.

20 Friedan, *The Feminine Mystique*, 301.

21 Friedan, *The Feminine Mystique*, 19, 337, 356.

22 Friedan, *The Feminine Mystique*, 342.

23 Friedan, *The Feminine Mystique*, 238. Friedan (*The Feminine Mystique*, 210) notes that, for example, Margaret Mead decried early marriage for boys because it stunted their intellectual growth and harmed society, but did not make the same argument in relation to girls.

24 Friedan, *The Feminine Mystique*, 329, 331, 341.

25 Friedan, *The Feminine Mystique*, 328–31, 357–8; Alfred Charles Kinsey et al., *Sexual Behavior in the Human Male* (Bloomington: Indiana University Press, 1949); Kinsey et al., *Sexual Behavior in the Human Female*.

26 Friedan, *The Feminine Mystique*, 328–9.

27 Kinsey met many of his homosexual subjects in bars and prisons; personal sexual interests and inclinations influenced his studies. See James H. Jones, *Alfred C. Kinsey: A Public/Private Life* (New York: W. W. Norton, 1997).

MODULE 7
ACHIEVEMENT

KEY POINTS

- Betty Friedan showed that postwar American society did not see women as people because the feminine mystique defined them through husbands and children and kept them from developing as individuals, to the detriment of all.

- She was able to make this point thanks to her academic training, interviews and questionnaires with women and families, and the availability of psychological, medical, and sociological reports.

- A sense of individual identity and purpose was achieved by women and men who worked alongside each other on the farms and plantations of the early United States — but just as women were ready to participate fully in the twentieth-century economy they were expected to devote their lives to unskilled housework.

Assessing The Argument

In *The Feminine Mystique*, Betty Friedan identifies the ways in which roles for middle-class women and men were created in the 1950s—and how they damaged everyone. She argues that the flight to the safety of suburban home and family life by young men and women prevents them from achieving adult individuality. This undermines their ability to be good parents and harms their relationship as a married couple.

For women the situation is far more serious because they are expected to give up educational and professional attainments in favor of complete "abdication of the self."[1] While experts understand the

> ❝ Why, with the removal of all the legal, political, economic, and educational barriers that once kept woman from being man's equal, a person in her own right, an individual free to develop her own potential, should she accept this new image which insists she is not a person but a 'woman,' by definition barred from the freedom of human existence and a voice in human destiny? ❞
>
> Betty Friedan, *The Feminine Mystique*

need for intellectual development and work in men, Friedan argues that they fail to recognize the same needs in women because of the "difference" that supposedly makes women content to strive vicariously through someone else.[2]

Friedan challenges the false equality of the feminine mystique, which makes housekeeping and childcare, finding bargains, and doing volunteer work a substitute for earning a living. True equality would give everyone the opportunity and expectation of educational and professional development in line with their abilities. This is the source of self-esteem and a fully developed individual identity. To support her case she brings in the American psychologist A. H. Maslow* on the hierarchy of needs.* Maslow argues that our need for personal and intellectual growth takes over when our basic biological needs are easily met, as they are for many in today's wealthy nations. Men are known to suffer when they are prevented from using their full mental capacities and achieving their potential—but the feminine mystique fixes women's destinies to the lower needs for sex and procreation.[3] Ironically, the stunting of growth in women prevents the transcendence of the self (that is, the move beyond self-interest) that allows for meaningful engagement with others, including husbands and children.[4]

Freidan argues that women need to take responsibility for their own choices, for "fulfilling their own unique possibilities as separate human beings."[5] She recognizes, however, how hard this can be once a woman has adjusted to being a housewife. Women cling to this ready-made identity in spite of the sense of nothingness, nonexistence, and emptiness it brings.[6] The feminine mystique is not just an individual problem—it is a national problem requiring social change.[7]

Achievement in Context

To explain how living under the feminine mystique makes women psychologically brittle and isolated, Friedan points to research showing that mindless, repetitive work beneath a worker's ability level results in the same frustrations and escapism seen in housewives.[8] Friedan also considers the effects of confined conditions and loss of individuality through the Austrian-born psychologist Bruno Bettelheim's* analysis of prisoners' behavior in Nazi concentration camps. He claimed to have witnessed this firsthand as a prisoner himself at the Dachau* and Buchenwald* concentration camps in 1939. Although Friedan pointedly states that housewives are not prisoners, she has been severely criticized for the comparison;[9] further, Bettelheim's portrayal of prisoners has since been called into question.[10]

Bettelheim explains the eerie indifference of prisoners in the face of death as the result less of brutality than of the routine they endured. On entering the camps, prisoners were stripped of their past interests and identities. Treated as children with no say over their use of time, they surrendered themselves into a faceless mass. Older prisoners were hostile to anyone who resisted the adjustment process they had already suffered through. The repetitive, mechanized work deprived prisoners of the use of their creativity and intellect. It was endless, fatiguing, and empty of meaning or recognition.[11] The loss of adult identity left prisoners intensely preoccupied with sex and other animal needs, but this inward focus interfered with meaningful relationships. Prisoners turned their rage upon each other instead of the guards. Friedan argues that housewifery likewise deprives women of adult identity and makes them passive, dependent, and childlike. They focus on food, sex, and objects, becoming "an anonymous biological robot in a docile mass," with no interest in the wider world because they no longer have any place in it.[12]

Friedan concludes with Bettelheim's story of a former dancer in a line of naked prisoners awaiting the gas chamber who was ordered to perform for the commanding officer. The woman approached him, took his gun, and shot him, for which she was instantly gunned down. Bettelheim reflects that being recalled to her previous self must have allowed the dancer to "throw off her real prison" in spite of the grotesque setting and the certainty of her own death.[13]

Limitations

Friedan has been criticized for concentrating on middle- and upper-class white women—but her core argument about the human need for identity and personal and intellectual growth transcends time and place.

Friedan makes her case through scientific knowledge that "the same range of potential ability exists for women as for men."[14] Furthermore, women do not constitute the biologically weaker sex.[15] She uses the psychoanalyst* Erik Erikson's* work on the central role of creative, socially purposeful work in men's growth and well-being to argue that the current economy is problematic for everyone's identity.

When work was done by women and men together for basic survival, as in the farms and plantations of the early United States, it was the solid basis for self-actualization* (psychological growth through sustained effort in education and work):[16] "Strength and independence, responsibility and self-confidence, self-discipline and courage, freedom and equality were part of the American character for both men and women, in all the first generations." This included

European immigrant couples who worked together in the urban economy.[17]

Comparing the United States to Europe, Friedan writes, "By an accident of history, American women shared in the work of society longer, and grew with the men."[18] Then women began to be excluded from the emerging industries and professions. The early feminists* understood that "education and the right to participate in the advanced work of society were women's greatest needs."[19]

Just when it was possible for women to "move on to something more," society expected them to devote themselves to unskilled housework.[20] The harmful effects of avoiding growth were recognized as pathological in boys but considered normal biological traits in girls. They were pushed into permanent dependence through a "mistaken choice between femaleness and humanness."[21] Similar choices—and the denial of opportunities to subordinated groups—reach far beyond the 1950s United States.

NOTES

1   Betty Friedan, *The Feminine Mystique* (New York: W. W. Norton & Company, 2013), 394.

2   Friedan, *The Feminine Mystique*, 393.

3   Friedan, *The Feminine Mystique*, 379–81, 392.

4   Friedan, *The Feminine Mystique*, 354–5.

5   Friedan, *The Feminine Mystique*, 406.

6   Friedan, *The Feminine Mystique*, 301.

7   Friedan, *The Feminine Mystique*, 439.

8   Friedan, *The Feminine Mystique*, 300.

9   See bell hooks, F*eminist Theory from Margin to Center* (Boston, MA: South End Press, 1984); Daniel Horowitz, *Betty Friedan and the Making of* The Feminine Mystique: *The American Left, the Cold War, and Modern Feminism* (Amherst: University of Massachusetts Press, 2000).

10 See Richard Pollak, *The Creation of Dr. B.: A Biography of Bruno Bettelheim* (New York: Simon & Schuster, 1997).

11 Friedan, *The Feminine Mystique*, 368.

12 Friedan, *The Feminine Mystique*, 370.

13 Friedan, *The Feminine Mystique*, 371.

14 Friedan, *The Feminine Mystique*, 405.

15 However, she notes that since taking up the 1950s housewife role, women "no longer live with the zest, the enjoyment, the sense of purpose that is characteristic of true human health." Friedan, *The Feminine Mystique*, 351.

16 Friedan, *The Feminine Mystique*, 402–3.

17 Friedan, *The Feminine Mystique*, 403–4.

18 Friedan, *The Feminine Mystique*, 404.

19 Friedan, *The Feminine Mystique*, 405.

20 Friedan, T*he Feminine Mystique*, 303.

21 Friedan, *The Feminine Mystique*, 365, also 342–3.

PLACE IN THE AUTHOR'S WORK

KEY POINTS

- Betty Friedan's life's work was to reveal how society interferes in women's educational and professional attainment through ideas, rules, and institutions that make femininity and individuality seem mutually exclusive.

- *The Feminine Mystique* was a powerful and impassioned analysis that established Friedan as an expert on beliefs concerning gender* held by middle-class Americans in the years following World War II.*

- The book established Friedan as a feminist* who avoided pitting women and men against each other, arguing instead that it was in everyone's interest to guarantee women access to economic and intellectual independence.

Positioning

Betty Friedan's *The Feminine Mystique* (1963) reveals just how thwarted, restless, and sick many American housewives were in the 1950s. In it, she argues that women have the same need for personal identity, growth, and socially purposeful work as men; if women are confined to a domestic existence, it is not because they are made any differently to men.

Friedan was able to identify the problem through her own experience as a wife and mother of the era. She had a taste of the life defined by the roles of housewife and breadwinner* for 10 years before starting on the book. She did not live completely as a housewife, however, continuing to work as a staff journalist and then a freelance writer following her marriage. She was also schooled before education

> **❝** And so the American woman ... ran back home again ... trading her individuality for security. Her husband was drawn in after her, and the door was shut against the outside world. They began to live the pretty lie of the feminine mystique, but could either of them really believe it? She was, after all, an American woman, an irreversible product of a culture that stops just short of giving her a separate identity. He was, after all, an American man whose respect for individuality and freedom of choice are his nation's pride. They went to school together; he knows who she is. **❞**
>
> Betty Friedan, *The Feminine Mystique*

became directed by gender-role* in the years following World War II. In fact, her research showed that women educated in her time had fewer problems living in the housewife role. They remained engaged with the wider world and continued to cultivate interests developed in college, even if they did not work for pay. Women who went to college later and often quit before finishing did not get the chance to develop a solid sense of self.[1] They were "doomed to suffer ultimately that bored, diffuse feeling of purposelessness, non-existence, non-involvement with the world" that can be felt as a lack of identity or what she termed "the problem that has no name."[2]

Friedan made it her life's work to help women out of the trap set by the feminine mystique. She considered it urgent. The damage increased through progressive generations and worsened over the lifetimes of individual women as they grew older. Husbands were frustrated by pressure from their wives for reflected glory and sexual attention. They disliked the simultaneously aggressive and dependent behavior that took the place of the sexual and motherly attention the mystique promised them. By pursuing magical fulfillment through marriage, women evaded their own growth and prevented their children from facing the tests of life. Society recognized the effect on boys, who are expected to endure the pains of growth, but Friedan shows the same should be expected of girls.[3]

Integration

Friedan argues that being trapped in a relentlessly repetitive existence is dehumanizing. As one mother put it, "I can take the real problems; it's the endless boring days that make me desperate."[4] What makes us human is the ability to see ahead, to understand the present through the past, to go beyond the boundaries of time and self. This is why working toward long-term aims and purposes is essential for productivity, relationships, and well-being—and why its absence affects all three.

In *The Feminine Mystique* Friedan uses her understanding of the problem to set out goals for women and society. Women must reject the feminine mystique with its unnecessary choice between femininity and individual personhood, family and career. A sense of self does not come through others or objects such as a house. It means keeping housework in its place (something to be finished in the most efficient way) and seeing that marriage is not a magical shortcut to self-realization (fulfilling one's own potential).

Women must tackle something that takes serious commitment and tests their abilities. This means paid work or education toward paid work that allows for individual creativity and contributes meaningfully to society.[5] Many women will be encouraged by husbands who see the benefit to their relationship and finances, but others must prepare for resistance. Unsupportive husbands, children, and fellow housewives, and religious and community leaders, will use whatever tools they can to stop them.[6]

Friedan's plan includes preventing education from being aimed at either girls or boys, and introducing practical help and incentives for adult students.[7] She calls for later marriage, which, along with education and work, will reduce the birthrate.[8] Friedan urges institutional and legal protections to ensure women's economic independence. This means having control of their own finances, as opposed to husbands controlling wives' money and men being the owners of houses and the only ones allowed to sign a lease or apply for a mortgage.

Finally, society must teach men not to fear competition at school and work. It is far less damaging than competition for dominance in the home.[9]

"And when women do not need to live through their husbands and children, men will not fear the love and strength of women, nor need another's weakness to prove their own masculinity. They can finally see each other as they are."[10]

Significance

The Feminine Mystique remains Friedan's most important and best-known book. Successive editions include an epilogue added in 1974 and an additional chapter in 1997. Her other books are all rooted in this first one. *It Changed My Life* (1976) discusses women's responses to *The Feminine Mystique*.[11] *The Second Stage* (1983) and *Beyond Gender* (1997) talk about the evolution of the women's movement.[12] *The Fountain of Age* (1993) tackles how the mystique makes old age a period of uselessness to dread. The book argues that strong relationships and contributions to the community make for long and interesting lives for both women and men.[13] Friedan's memoir, *Life So Far* (2000), looks back on her role in twentieth-century feminism.[14]

Throughout her work Friedan presents herself as an ordinary, if well educated, housewife and mother who also wrote for women's magazines.[15] Her reluctance to discuss her involvement in labor union activism and leftist publications is understandable in light of the times.[16] The prominent politician Joseph McCarthy led an investigation of suspected communists aggressive enough to blight the careers of many actors, writers, and directors (among others). McCarthyism* in the 1950s targeted union activists and educators for signs of communist sympathies. Friedan's book might never have been published if she had looked at the question from an explicitly political perspective, or acknowledged leftist influences on her thinking.[17]

Friedan's reputation does not rest upon her writings alone. She cofounded the National Organization for Women (NOW)* and served as its president until 1970. She promoted women's rights to educational and professional opportunities, equal treatment in the workplace, and a fair position in society and the family. She chose a moderate approach in a bid to maintain dialogue and camaraderie among women and between women and men.[18]

NOTES

1 Betty Friedan, *The Feminine Mystique* (New York: W. W. Norton & Company, 2013), 431–6.

2 Friedan, *The Feminine Mystique*, 211.

3 Friedan, *The Feminine Mystique*, 210, 366.

4 Friedan, *The Feminine Mystique*, 377.

5 Friedan, *The Feminine Mystique*, 403, 416, 419.

6 Friedan, *The Feminine Mystique*, 424–8.

7 Friedan, *The Feminine Mystique*, 436, 446–8.

8 Friedan, *The Feminine Mystique*, 465.

9 Friedan, *The Feminine Mystique*, 451.

10 Friedan, *The Feminine Mystique*, 456.

11 Betty Friedan, *"It Changed My Life": Writings on the Women's Movement* (Cambridge, MA: Harvard University Press, 1998).

12 Betty Friedan, *The Second Stage* (New York: Simon & Schuster, 1981); Betty Friedan, *Beyond Gender: The New Politics of Work and Family* (Washington, DC: Woodrow Wilson Center Press, 1997).

13 Betty Friedan, *The Fountain of Age* (New York: Simon & Schuster, 2006).

14 Betty Friedan, *Life So Far: A Memoir* (New York: Simon & Schuster, 2000).

15 See Daniel Horowitz, *Betty Friedan and the Making of* The Feminine Mystique: *The American Left, the Cold War, and Modern Feminism* (Amherst: University of Massachusetts Press, 2000).

16 See Horowitz, *Betty Friedan*, xii.

17 Stefanie Coontz, A *Strange Stirring: The Feminine Mystique and American Women at the Dawn of the 1960s* (New York: Basic Books, 2011), 66, 143.

18 Friedan, *The Feminine Mystique*, 468–74.

SECTION 3
IMPACT

THE FIRST RESPONSES

KEY POINTS

- Though *The Feminine Mystique* became a best-selling book, it sparked outrage and derision for questioning conventional male and female roles in 1950s America.

- Betty Friedan responded by becoming increasingly frustrated with the pace of social and political change, using the fame her book brought her to attract activists and influence policymakers.

- The book's reception echoed the experiences of an earlier generation of feminists* who had highlighted inequalities in the nineteenth century, and Friedan galvanized a women's movement that had fallen quiet after World War I*—even though many women were politically active and employed in industry and government.

Criticism

Betty Friedan's *The Feminine Mystique* sold three million copies in the first three years.[1] Although Friedan was swamped with letters from women inspired and empowered by her best-selling book, she also faced a storm of hostile criticism. Before publication, magazines including *McCall's, Ladies' Home Journal*, and *Redbook* had rejected an article Friedan wrote on the subject.[2] However, the publisher, W. W. Norton, went ahead despite resistance from within the company.[3]

Newspaper articles attacked *The Feminine Mystique* and its author's femininity together. Friedan was scorned for trying to emasculate men and leave millions on the street.[4] Professional ambitions seen as worthy in men became a frivolous need to "find themselves" in women. Housewives were chastised for not appreciating their easy,

> **❝** It is my thesis that the core of the problem for women today is not sexual but a problem of identity—a stunting or evasion of growth that is perpetuated by the feminine mystique. It is my thesis that as the Victorian culture did not permit women to accept or gratify their basic sexual needs, our culture does not permit women to accept or gratify their basic need to grow and fulfill their potentialities as human beings, a need which is not solely defined by their sexual role. **❞**
>
> Betty Friedan, *The Feminine Mystique*

well-off lifestyles—the envy of women the world over who slaved away in factories, agriculture, and dirty, physically demanding housework. Jokes and cartoons in mainstream publications including the *Wall Street Journal* mocked the very idea of women in "masculine" professions or leadership positions.[5]

The criticism did not stop Friedan. In the mid-1960s, she joined forces with women working in government, business, unions, and the media to press for political changes affecting women. They founded the National Organization for Women (NOW)* in 1966 in frustration over nonenforcement of the 1964 Civil Rights Act,* which newspapers including the *New York Times* blatantly violated with gender-specific job ads.[6] Friedan helped form the National Women's Political Caucus* that (unsuccessfully) pressed Congress to approve the Equal Rights Amendment* a half-century after it was first proposed. Friedan, the writer Gloria Steinem,* and the politician Bella Abzug* called the Women's Strike for Equality* to celebrate the 50th anniversary of the women's suffrage* amendment (the passing of a law that guaranteed women the right to vote).[7] That 1970 march through New York City suddenly made it "both political and glamorous to be a feminist."[8]

Responses

To understand the book's reception we must first acknowledge the state of play for women in the 1960s. For a start, powerful women were not part of the landscape of popular culture, especially white middle-class women. "Black women civil rights leaders spoke out, faced down mobs, and braved jail, but the only women regularly featured in the news were movie stars and presidents' wives, who were always described by their outfits."[9] Female college professors were so rare that the feminist Jo Freeman,* who became a leader of the women's movement in the 1960s and 1970s, never saw one in her four years at Berkeley* and "worse yet, I didn't notice."[10]

Women's wages were half of men's, according to a 1965 report by the President's Commission on the Status of Women. The proportion of women in professional and executive jobs was in decline.[11] The report included recommendations for measures to help working women and increase their access to high-level positions. But its introduction, written by the anthropologist* Margaret Mead,* contradicted them by asking who would tend the husbands and children.[12]

In most states in the early 1960s, women could not take out a loan without a male cosigner. In some states, husbands owned their wives' property and earnings. Some states excluded women from jury service. Newspaper job listings were separated by sex, and employers including the federal government could exclude women from consideration.[13] In 1965, the Supreme Court ruled that married women could not be denied contraceptives, but unmarried women had to wait until 1972 to have the right to access contraception. Abortion was illegal except to save the mother's life. In some American states it was illegal for women to wear men's clothing.[14] This was the status quo that Friedan boldly challenged with *The Feminine Mystique*, so the reaction was predictably hostile.

Conflict and Consensus

The fury of the book's early critics recalls the attacks on nineteenth-century feminists. They rebelled against a culture that for centuries had doubted the very existence of a female soul or fully evolved brain and had deprived women of legal and economic independence. Denied a place at antislavery rallies, women including Elizabeth Stanton* and Lucretia Mott* organized the First Women's Rights Convention in Seneca Falls, New York, in 1848. Speaking out against woman's unrecognized enslavement through institutions including marriage and property laws, they explained how man has "endeavored in every way that he could to destroy her confidence in her own powers, to lessen her self-respect, and to make her willing to lead a dependent and abject life."[15]

In spite of fierce opposition, early feminists fought for inclusion in the new urban, industrial economy. They bridled against the view of women as fixed and unchanging, apparently anchored by their anatomy, while men were permitted to change with the times.[16] Friedan observes that the struggle transformed them into "a different kind of woman. They became complete human beings."[17] Many men were on their side, including the husband of the abolitionist Lucy Stone* (an abolitionist is someone opposed to the institution of slavery). Educated at Oberlin College,* the first higher education institution in the United States to regularly enroll women and minority students, Stone kept her own name and, therefore, her legal existence after marriage. Their minister sent the couple's vows to the local newspapers; Friedan quotes him writing, "I never perform the marriage ceremony without a renewed sense of the iniquity of a system by which man and wife are one, and that one is the husband."[18]

Friedan spoke out against society's return to this conventional view of men and women in society after all that had been gained by First Wave* feminists of the nineteenth and early twentieth century. *The Feminine Mystique* shattered the dormant phase of feminism that began after World War I and left no doubt that much remained to be done.[19] The heated response to her work exposed the insidious power of the feminine mystique. The book was ridiculed because its author was a woman and therefore not a credible authority.

NOTES

1   Public Broadcasting Service, "Betty Friedan and *The Feminine Mystique*," accessed 31 October 2015, www.pbs.org/fmc/segments/progseg11.htm.

2   Betty Friedan, *The Feminine Mystique* (New York: W. W. Norton & Company, 2013), 513–14.

3   Jennifer Scheussler, "Criticisms of a Classic Unbound," *New York Times*, February 18, 2013.

4   Stefanie Coontz, *A Strange Stirring:* The Feminine Mystique *and American Women at the Dawn of the 1960s* (New York: Basic Books, 2011), 31.

5   Coontz, *A Strange Stirring*, 155.

6   Coontz, *A Strange Stirring*, 17.

7   Friedan, *The Feminine Mystique*, 467, 473.

8   Friedan, *The Feminine Mystique*, 471.

9   Coontz, *A Strange Stirring*, 17.

10 In Coontz, *A Strange Stirring*, 17.

11 Friedan, *The Feminine Mystique*, 460.

12 Friedan, *The Feminine Mystique*, 460–1.

13 Gail Collins, "Introduction," in The Feminine Mystique, by Betty Friedan (New York: W. W. Norton & Company, 2013), xii.

14 Coontz, *A Strange Stirring*, 11.

15 In Friedan, *The Feminine Mystique*, 86.

16 Friedan, *The Feminine Mystique*, 82.

17 Friedan, *The Feminine Mystique*, 91.

18 Friedan, *The Feminine Mystique*, 93.

19 Coontz, *A Strange Stirring*, 66.

THE EVOLVING DEBATE

KEY POINTS

- Key concepts set out in *The Feminine Mystique* helped to shape the feminist* movement's aims and actions in the 1970s and beyond by emphasizing the need to change how society views women's roles and abilities.

- Betty Friedan helped to lead a Second Wave* of feminism in the United States, winning major changes in women's reproductive rights, economic and legal independence, and treatment in the home and workplace.

- She did not see men as the enemy, skirted the issue of domestic violence, and disliked graphic sexual or antimarriage and antimotherhood rhetoric—stances that distanced her from more radical feminists.

Uses And Problems

Betty Friedan's *The Feminine Mystique* had a huge impact on the Second Wave feminist movement of the 1960s to the 1980s (the First Wave* began in the nineteenth century), giving the movement strength and direction by exposing for the fictions they were mainstream beliefs that domestic drudgery was somehow glorious. Change was slow at first. American schoolgirls continued to be taught the techniques of homemaking and feminine self-effacement (modesty) until well into the 1970s.[1] At that time the National Organization for Women* had only 3,000 members in 30 cities.[2] Friedan reports that although nearly half of all American women worked outside the home, they felt guilty about neglecting their families.[3]

However, by the mid-1970s Friedan had reason for satisfaction and

> ❝ Grown-up men and women, no longer obsessed with youth, outgrowing finally children's games, and obsolete rituals of power and sex, become more and more authentically themselves. And they do not pretend that men are from Mars or women are from Venus. They even share each other's interests; talk common shorthand of work, love, play, kids, politics. We may now begin to glimpse the new human possibilities when women and men are finally free to be themselves, know each other for who they really are, and define the terms and measures of success, failure, joy, triumph, power, and the common good, together. ❞
>
> Betty Friedan, *The Feminine Mystique*

optimism. The Supreme Court had ruled that no state could deny women the right to choose to end an unwanted pregnancy. Universities and businesses were being forced by lawsuits to take action over gender* discrimination.[4] It was becoming harder for employers to fire women for being married or growing older. Airlines could no longer force flight attendants to retire when they married or arrived at the age of 30, for example.[5] Birth rates and divorce rates were down. Women's movements had taken off around the world, and women's studies had become an academic discipline.[6]

By the mid-1990s there was more reporting of sexual abuse, domestic violence, and harassment. Three-fifths of women worked outside the home (nearly half the labor force), although they earned 25 per cent less than men.[7] Title 9 of the Civil Rights Act* prohibited discrimination by sex* in education, including athletics. Couples were having sex more often and enjoying it more.[8] Research showed that combining work and family was beneficial to women and that the menopause no longer brought a decline in mental health.[9]

On the other hand, there were threats to women's legally recognized reproductive rights. Corporate greed and downsizing led to stagnant or declining wages and a growing gap between rich and poor.[10] Friedan worried that "a backlash from the men, egged on by the media and political hatemongers" could "make scapegoats of women again."[11]

Schools of Thought

Following the book's publication, Friedan continued to write for women's magazines including *Ladies' Home Journal* and *McCall's*;[12] she added an epilogue to the book a decade later, and another chapter in 1997. These pieces and her second book on women's responses to the first[13] reveal an enormous softening of her rhetoric and a weakening of the passion that energizes *The Feminine Mystique.*

For instance, Friedan reins in her criticism of housewifery and attempts to write supportively of some women's choice to pursue an exclusively domestic career.[14] She argues that women's work inside the home has economic value that should be accounted for in the calculation of retirement benefits;[15] also that voluntary associations are crucial to communities, that society has begun to recognize their importance, and that their future depends on the cultivation of "bonds of civic engagement."[16] These changes clearly address the "strange hostility" Friedan observed in some women, though she must have expected it.[17] In *The Feminine Mystique*, Friedan contrasts the isolating self-contempt of women who did not join the nineteenth-century feminist movement against the camaraderie amongst feminists and their solidarity with all women.[18]

While arguing that further progress will be made when men "break through to a new way of thinking about themselves and society,"[19] Friedan makes every effort not to alienate them. She writes that from the start men did not express the resistance she expected. Both men and women saw the possibilities in moving beyond the feminine mystique. "I've seen great relief in women … as I've spelled out my personal truth: that the assumption of your own identity, equality, and even political power does not mean you stop needing to love, and be loved by, a man, or that you stop caring for your kids."[20] These statements reflect Friedan's vision of a women's movement based on conventional female–male relationships and point to the problems ahead.

In Current Scholarship

Friedan does not see men as the enemy, but rather "fellow victims, suffering from an outmoded masculine mystique." [21] This idea has its merits but also its problems. It lets individual men off the hook for resisting the loss of the privileges they enjoy when women are defined as a servant class. Men are also excused for the formidable barriers they put in the way of women's independence. Paradoxically, while sparing men from individual responsibility, Friedan urges women to break the chains of the feminine mystique on their own—despite recognizing how hard this was for her. Speaking of her divorce, Friedan writes, "It was easier for me to start the women's movement which was needed to change society than to change my own personal life."[22]

While Friedan discusses parental violence against children in *The Feminine Mystique*, she skirts the issue of men's violent rage against women. The chapter she added to the book in 1997 notes that increased rates of domestic violence are likely to be due at least in part to men's rage against late-twentieth-century economic constriction.[23] This accommodating attitude toward men set Friedan apart from other feminists and scholars, who showed that domestic violence is the predictable result of factors including cultural beliefs about women's inferiority, structural conditions limiting women's economic independence, and women's isolation from family and other support networks.[24]

Friedan resisted what she saw as counterproductive or unseemly strains of Second Wave feminism in the 1970s and 1980s. These included "man-hating" antimarriage and antimotherhood rhetoric, the ideology of sex warfare based on analogies to race and class struggles, and a provocative, graphic focus on sex organs and sex acts as a revolt against women's longtime objectification.[25] Contrary to Friedan's expectations, more radical thought grew in importance, ushering in a Third Wave* of feminism beginning in the late 1980s.[26]

NOTES

1 See, for example, Marion S. Barclay and Frances Champion, *Teen Guide to Homemaking* (New York: McGraw-Hill, 1967).

2 Betty Friedan, *The Feminine Mystique* (New York: W. W. Norton & Company, 2013), 470.

3 Friedan, *The Feminine Mystique*, 512.

4 Friedan, *The Feminine Mystique*, 473.

5 Friedan, *The Feminine Mystique*, 466, 474.

6 Friedan, *The Feminine Mystique*, 468.

7 Friedan, *The Feminine Mystique*, 489.

8 Friedan, *The Feminine Mystique*, 496.

9 Friedan, *The Feminine Mystique*, 497.

10 Friedan, *The Feminine Mystique*, 487, 488, 490, 491.

11 Friedan, *The Feminine Mystique*, 489.

12 Friedan, *The Feminine Mystique*, 475.

13 Betty Friedan, *"It Changed My Life": Writings on the Women's Movement* (Cambridge, MA: Harvard University Press, 1998).

14 Anna Quindlen, "Afterword," in *The Feminine Mystique*, by Betty Friedan (New York: W. W. Norton & Company, 2013), 481.

15 Friedan, *The Feminine Mystique*, 464.

16 Friedan, *The Feminine Mystique*, 41.

17 Friedan, *The Feminine Mystique*, 459.

18 Friedan, *The Feminine Mystique*, 107.

19 Friedan, *The Feminine Mystique*, 485.

20 Friedan, *The Feminine Mystique*, 476.

21 Friedan, *The Feminine Mystique*, 465.

22 Friedan, *The Feminine Mystique*, 459.

23 Friedan, *The Feminine Mystique*, 493.

24 Lori L. Heise, "Violence, Sexuality, and Women's Lives," in *The Gender/ Sexuality Reader*, ed. Roger N. Lancaster and Micaela di Leonardo (New York: Routledge, 1997), 411–33.

25 Friedan, *The Feminine Mystique*, 468–70.

26 Friedan, *The Feminine Mystique*, 474.

MODULE 11
IMPACT AND INFLUENCE TODAY

KEY POINTS

- While *The Feminine Mystique* is considered a classic Second Wave* feminist* text, there is still a good deal of debate over how honest Betty Friedan was about her background and whether her work focused on an unrepresentative and narrow group of women.

- Though hugely influential in reviving the feminist movement in the 1960s and 1970s, Friedan was not the only person challenging traditional gender* roles and tended to gloss over the achievements of women in public life to make her case in the book.

- Modern-day feminist thinkers and activists have built on the social changes sparked in part by Friedan's text by exploring the performativity* of gender (roughly, acting a role until it becomes real) and realities of alternative sexualities and genders.

Position

From the very start, Betty Friedan's The Feminine Mystique has been criticized for its focus on middle-class white women. On the other hand, Friedan's writing and activism involved tireless work to improve the lot of all women, including African Americans subjected to the combined force of sexism and racism and the working-class women the book "is always criticized for ignoring."[1] As a journalist, Friedan reported on and was inspired by working-class women trade unionists during and after World War II.*[2]

Friedan also stands accused of exaggerating the originality of her analysis and underplaying women's participation in business and

> **❝ We do not fight with man himself, but only with bad principles. ❞**
>
> Ernestine Rose,* quoted by Betty Friedan in *The Feminine Mystique*

government at the time. This can partly be explained by her need to keep a low political profile in the era of McCarthyism* (named for the aggressively anticommunist politician Joseph McCarthy, when being investigated as a suspected communist could wreck a career). She did not discuss her involvement with unions and leftist publications in the 1940s, or her interest in radical thinkers such as the German economists and political philosophers Karl Marx* and Friedrich Engels* in college.[3]

Friedan also failed to give credit to other sources for her ideas. These include the learned rather than inborn nature of gender roles, the psychological damage of forced domesticity, and the harmful effects down the generations of all-consuming motherhood.[4] Only some of these sources would have been political hot potatoes at the time, such as the periodical Harper's and intellectual Simone de Beauvoir.*[5]

Friedan's self-portrait as an ordinary housewife protected her from accusations of leftist sympathies, made her accomplishments more impressive, and allowed her to claim to represent the average woman. Whether a well-intended narrative strategy or the deliberate lie proposed by critics including the American Studies scholar Daniel Horowitz* and the political scientist Alan Wolfe,* the idea that she was an isolated woman whose ideas came through a unique personal evolution supported her insistence that any woman could change her life through willpower.[6] This personal angle allowed Friedan to argue also for changed institutions and a revolution in gender roles.[7]

Interaction

Friedan's efforts on behalf of all women paradoxically led her to the same tendency to define them in terms of their sex that she criticized in *The Feminine Mystique*. In reality, between 1945 and 1960 women had identities that combined class, ethnicity, occupation, political and religious affiliation, and sexuality in a variety of ways.* Contrary to Friedan's portrait of women's magazines, career women often appeared in their pages—although squarely within prevailing standards of femininity.[8]

Women were already challenging traditional gender roles, and were not absent from politics or government in the 1950s. Friedan did not start the Second Wave feminist movement, as she and others claimed.[9] Friedan says that 1950s pollsters and candidates did not consider women because they just voted with their husbands.[10] In reality, the National Woman's Party* and the National Federation of Business and Professional Women's Clubs* had pressured President Eisenhower* in 1956 to ask Congress for an (unsuccessful) equal pay for equal work measure. Eisenhower was eager to attract the "women's vote," and increased the number of female political appointees. President Kennedy,* Eisenhower's successor, likewise understood the political value of women's support.[11]

Friedan's book was one of the sparks contributing to the gradual growth of the revived feminist movement in the 1960s and its subsequent explosion in the 1970s. The movement empowered women and brought enormous institutional changes in employment, education, and reproductive rights. Eventually, however, the lack of attention to the impact of factors such as politics, personal roots, and class on their thinking created a divide between 1970s feminists and the generations that followed.

The Continuing Debate

In the 1980s, scholars and critics shifted attention away from women as a class united by a common and obvious cause (such as sexist laws). Instead, they discussed the wide variety of female circumstances, identities, and viewpoints.[12] The feminist writer bell hooks* criticized Friedan for self-indulgently and sensationally recounting the malaise of educated, white, leisure-class women without considering the effects of sexism on women such as the housecleaning and childcare workers whose labor is necessary for the middle-class women to pursue careers.[13]

The literary theorist Judith Butler* questioned the words used to categorize people and create and reinforce inequalities, exploring how gender rules and expectations affect people in everyday interaction.[14] Her theory rested on the idea that people "perform" society's gender expectations, thereby creating themselves as gendered beings. In the early 1990s, feminist author Rebecca Walker* gave the name "Third Wave Feminism"* to the strands of feminism unified by a shared rejection of blanket concepts of femininity.[15]

Friedan predicts this shift in *The Feminine Mystique* through arguments about individual identity and self-actualization* (the development and continued exercise of individual abilities through training and work). Yet she remained a Second Wave feminist. She did not embrace the flowering of interest in multiple sexualities and genders that began in the late 1960s, and initially was openly resistant to the growing influence of lesbian feminists.[16] She did, however, abandon the negative view of homosexuality that had led her to equate it with an immature personality, possibly caused by overactive parenting. A decade later, Friedan acknowledged the legitimacy and importance of alternatives to conventional heterosexual relationships and identities.[17] By the 1990s, she wrote in appreciation of diversity and new ways of organizing relationships and families, saying this was good for children.[18]

Friedan worked within the assumptions of a society that gave higher status to areas of life designated as male, leading her to argue that access to them was the key to improving women's status. She saw same-sex education as "a temporary obsolete timidity."[19] Her dim view of breastfeeding dispensed with a practice that is extremely beneficial to infants and mothers, and created another false choice for women—a choice between breastfeeding and work that would not exist if men took on more domestic responsibility or society valued motherhood.[20] Third Wave feminists are able to approach these issues through different perspectives thanks to the social changes brought about by Friedan's generation.

NOTES

1 Gail Collins, "Introduction," in *The Feminine Mystique*, by Betty Friedan (New York: W. W. Norton & Company, 2013), xix.

2 Daniel Horowitz, *Betty Friedan and the Making of* The Feminine Mystique: *The American Left, the Cold War, and Modern Feminism* (Amherst: University of Massachusetts Press, 2000), xii.

3 Stefanie Coontz, *A Strange Stirring: the Feminine Mystique and American Women at the Dawn of the 1960s* (New York: Basic Books, 2011), 66, 143.

4 Coontz, *A Strange Stirring*, 48.

5 Friedan maintained her silence to the end, only acknowledging her labor union involvement in her 2000 memoir: Betty Friedan, *Life So Far: A Memoir* (New York: Simon & Schuster, 2000); Horowitz, *Betty Friedan and the Making of* The Feminine Mystique, xii.

6 Horowitz, *Betty Friedan and the Making of* The Feminine Mystique; Alan Wolfe, "The Mystique of Betty Friedan," *The Atlantic* 284, no. 3 (1999): 98–105.

7 Betty Friedan, *The Feminine Mystique* (New York: W. W. Norton & Company, 2013), 463.

8 Joanne Meyerowitz, ed., *Not June Cleaver: Women and Gender in Postwar America 1945–1960* (Philadelphia: Temple University Press, 1994).

9 Coontz, *A Strange Stirring*, 139, 143.

10 Friedan, *The Feminine Mystique*, 487.

11 Coontz, *A Strange Stirring*, 150.

12 bell hooks, *Ain't I a Woman? Black Women and Feminism* (Boston, MA: South End Press, 1981); bell hooks, *We Real Cool: Black Men and Masculinity* (New York: Routledge, 2004).

13 bell hooks, *Feminist Theory from Margin to Center* (Boston, MA: South End Press, 1984).

14 Judith Butler, *Gender Trouble: Feminism and the Subversion of Identity* (New York: Routledge, 1990); *Judith Butler, Bodies that Matter: On the Discursive Limits of "Sex"* (New York: Routledge, 1993).

15 Rebecca Walker, ed., *To Be Real: Telling the Truth and Changing the Face of Feminism* (New York: Anchor Books, 1995); Jennifer Baumgardner and Amy Richards, *Manifesta: Young Women, Feminism, and the Future* (New York: Farrar, Strauss, and Giroux, 2000).

16 See Rachel Bowlby, *Still Crazy After All These Years: Women, Writing, and Psychoanalysis* (New York: Routledge, 1992).

17 Friedan, *The Feminine Mystique*, 329.

18 See Friedan, *The Feminine Mystique*, 498.

19 Friedan, *The Feminine Mystique*, 505.

20 Friedan, *The Feminine Mystique*, 167, 180; see Patricia Stuart-Macadam and Katherine Dettwyler, eds, *Breastfeeding: Biocultural Perspectives* (New York: Aldine de Gruyter, 1995).

WHERE NEXT?

KEY POINTS

- *The Feminine Mystique* remains an influential text for its lucid description of postwar America, how ideas about gender* roles fit with socioeconomic conditions, and the heavy costs of preventing women from achieving their potential.

- Betty Friedan identified and helped to eliminate the false choice between femininity and individuality, paving the way for a new generation of feminists to tackle issues such as the language and meaning of gender.

- More than 50 years after publication, Betty Friedan's seminal work is still relevant to debates around new obstacles to education and opportunity (including theories about the female brain) and women's place in domestic life and consumer culture.

Potential

In *The Feminine Mystique*, Betty Friedan argues that women—like men— should be seen as people above all else. To her generation of feminists, once the institutional framework was set right nothing would get in the way of women concerning individual growth and identity. Second Wave* feminism brought about enormous changes to the laws and social institutions of the United States—yet male dominance persists in less visible forms, putting limits on the lives of women.

In her later work Friedan notes that women are still kept out of top jobs through subtle forms of discrimination. She laments the conservative politics that aims to restrict women's autonomy in terms

> ❝ In education, in marriage, in religion, in everything, disappointment is the lot of woman. It shall be the business of my life to deepen this disappointment in every woman's heart until she bows down to it no longer. ❞
>
> Robert D. Putnam, *Bowling Alone*

of reproductive rights, divorce, and support for children, students, and the elderly.[1] Friedan argues for shorter workdays for all, so that both parents can balance careers and family.[2] Echoing the housewife's cry in *The Feminine Mystique*, Friedan asks, "When will men turn on the culture of greed and say, 'Is this all?'"[3]

Friedan never questions, however, the way domestic life is linked to femininity and work while politics is linked to masculinity. She attributes changes in the legislative agenda on families, relationships, and caregiving to the increased presence of women in politics and government. In this way she buys into the supposed division between the public (masculine) and private (feminine) spheres, as if relationships and caregiving were the concern of women only.[4]

While she argues against the isolated mother–child unit as a flawed and damaging model for parenting, she also takes for granted women's primary responsibility for children.[5] Although Friedan regrets the existence of a masculine mystique equating manhood with economic performance, her awareness that American society grants more prestige to the world of work leaves her arguing more forcefully for women's paid work than men's domestic work.[6] This makes her perspective a problem for younger generations of women.

Future Directions

The Feminine Mystique is rooted in the idea that women are united by a shared need to be permitted to become individuals. Later feminists question the basis for identifying individuals as women in the first place. This Third Wave* (the name for the feminist current active from the late 1980s) encompasses a varied and complex set of viewpoints and is so decentered that many such feminists are reluctant to identify themselves as part of a unified movement. Third Wave feminism has generated its own backlashes, including what Friedan describes as "outmoded, stunted, brutal youth-arrested machismo," and a new "feminine protest"—young women's refusal to identify with feminism.[7]

Friedan's message has come full circle in the work of Amy Richards,* who cofounded the Third Wave Foundation* with fellow writer Rebecca Walker* in 1992. After years of activism and feminist work on sexuality* and gender, Richards has written about motherhood. Her 2008 book is *Opting In: Having a Child without Losing Yourself.*[8]

Third Wave feminists no longer face the false and unnecessary choice between femininity and individuality identified by Friedan. That change is thanks to the work of First and Second Wave feminists, along with Third Wave challenges to the language of gender and power.

These waves are not separate phases—just as women's roles and social position have not followed the simple line Friedan envisioned, despite the anthropologist* Margaret Mead's* 1930s work showing that gender roles vary dramatically across societies and that women are not everywhere dominated by men. The issues circle back upon themselves, and gender beliefs and roles change in many directions. The different types of feminism that exist today are another form of resistance to concepts such as the feminine mystique, used to suggest that there is a single essence of female experience. They reflect the on-the-ground variability in women's identities and life experiences across cultures and times, including the period analyzed by Friedan.

Summary

Friedan points out that when she was writing *The Feminine Mystique*, people claimed the battle for women's rights had already been won.[9] Today the same idea underpins the concept of a postfeminist era. Yet the problem Friedan identified—that women are not counted as persons—remains unsolved.

There are new barriers to education and employment, such as claims about gender differences in specific cognitive (mental) abilities related to math and science. These create anxieties that suppress performance and end up reinforcing stereotypes.[10]

Femininity is still used to sell things, from consumer products to the campaign against breast cancer (as opposed to more common causes of sickness and death in women such as lung cancer and cardiovascular disease).[11] At conferences and book presentations accomplished women are questioned about having children, their happiness cast in doubt if they have not experienced motherhood.[12]

Mainstream films and television shows portray women in the happy homemaker role, although some such as the US television series *Mad Men*,* set primarily in the 1960s, and the film *I Smile Back** explore female depression, substance abuse, and lack of marital and sexual satisfaction.[13]

Global economic and political instability in the early twenty-first century has generated a new retreat into consumerism and domestic life.[14] Exactly as in other times of gender competition in the workplace, women are told that children should be raised by full-time mothers. This is in spite of the weight of evidence showing that work outside the home benefits both woman and child.[15]

Social commentators including certain feminists such as Camille Paglia* insist that women's biological sexuality is the ultimate source of both their power and vulnerability.[16] In a new form of the feminine mystique, homemaking is defined as a job and conducted with the earnestness of a career. Teachers and other educators complain of an epidemic of overprotective and interfering "helicopter parents" who relentlessly insert themselves into their children's schools and activities, and whose children fall apart at college.[17] More than 50 years after her landmark book appeared, such modern issues resonate with the world described by Friedan—and ensure the continued relevance of her ideas.

NOTES

1   Betty Friedan, *The Feminine Mystique* (New York: W. W. Norton & Company, 2013), 494.

2   Friedan, *The Feminine Mystique*, 490–1.

3   Friedan, *The Feminine Mystique*, 499.

4   Friedan, *The Feminine Mystique*, 494, 508.

5   In the book, Friedan assumes that full-time university studies are impossible for mothers of small children: Friedan, *The Feminine Mystique*, 497.

6   Friedan, *The Feminine Mystique*, 465.

7   Friedan, *The Feminine Mystique*, 493.

8   Amy Richards, *Opting In: Having a Child without Losing Yourself* (New York: Farrar, Straus, and Giroux, 2008).

9   Friedan, *The Feminine Mystique*, 452.

10 Steven J. Spencer et al., "Stereotype Threat and Women's Math Performance," *Journal of Experimental Social Psychology* 35 (1999): 4–28.

11 Friedan, *The Feminine Mystique*, 504; Barbara Ehrenreich, *Bright-Sided: How Positive Thinking is Undermining America* (New York: Picador, 2009).

12 Rebecca Solnit, "The Mother of All Questions," *Harper's* 331, no. 1985 (2015): 5–7.

13 *Mad Men* is a series created by Matthew Reiner and produced by Lionsgate Television that ran from 2007 to 2015; *I Smile Back* is a 2015 film directed by Adam Salky and produced by Egoli Tossell Film and Koppelman/Levien.

14 See Gail Collins, "Introduction," in *The Feminine Mystique*, by Betty Friedan (New York: W. W. Norton & Company, 2013), xiv.

15 Emily Martin, *The Woman in the Body: A Cultural Analysis of Reproduction* (Boston, MA: Beacon Press, 1987); Rachel G. Lucas-Thompson et al., "Maternal Work Early in the Lives of Children and its Distal Associations with Achievement and Behavior Problems: a Meta-Analysis," *Psychological Bulletin* 136, no. 6 (2010): 915–42; Adrianne Frech and Sarah Damaske, "The Relationships between Mothers' Work Pathways and Physical and Mental Health," *Journal of Health and Social Behavior* 53, no. 4 (2012): 396–412.

16 Camille Paglia, "The Modern Campus Cannot Comprehend Evil," *Time*, September 29, 2014, accessed October 31, 2015, http://time. com/3444749/camille-paglia-the-modern-campus-cannot-comprehend-evil/.

17 Julie Lythcott-Haims, *How to Raise an Adult: Break Free of the Overparenting Trap and Prepare Your Kids for Success* (New York: Henry Holt & Co., 2015).

GLOSSARY

GLOSSARY OF TERMS

Anthropology: the study of the biological and cultural history and current variability of humankind.

Breadwinner: a person who earns all or the majority of the income on which family members depend.

Buchenwald: a town in central Germany where there was a Nazi concentration camp from 1937 until 1945.

Civil Rights Act: legislation enacted in 1964 by the 88th US Congress that made discrimination by race, sex, religion, and national origin illegal in the workplace, public schools, voter registration practices, and public facilities.

Columbia University: an American private Ivy League research university founded in 1754 in New York City, consisting of 20 schools and many research institutes throughout the world.

Dachau: a city in southeastern Germany and site of a Nazi concentration camp from 1933 until 1945.

Developmental psychologist: a researcher or mental health professional trained in the branch of psychology focused on behavioral changes across the life cycle.

Equal Rights Amendment: a proposed amendment to the US Constitution to guarantee equal rights for women, first introduced in 1923 and nearly ratified in the 1970s.

Eugenics: the study of biological inheritance for the purpose of improving the quality of the human race through selective breeding and controlled reproduction.

Fascism: an authoritarian system of government founded by Benito Mussolini in Italy in 1919, involving strong state control of the economy, suppression of political dissent, and patriotic nationalism; the inspiration for similar nationalist movements in Europe, including Germany.

Feminism: a word denoting the various political, cultural, and intellectual currents associated with the struggle for equality between the sexes.

First Wave feminism: the worldwide late nineteenth- and early twentieth-century women's movement concentrated in the UK, US, Canada, the Netherlands, and Sweden, with a focus on legal reform and particularly women's suffrage.

Functionalism: an approach stressing utility and practicality, according to which the purpose of an object determines its characteristics. In social sciences, the view that societies are made up of interdependent systems that are analogous to those of the human body and which work together to maintain a steady state.

Gender: a social and cultural designation by which humans are classified as women, men, or other categories more or less loosely related to biological sex.

Great Depression: the worldwide economic downturn of the 1930s, characterized by unemployment, falling prices, and reduced production.

Hierarchy of needs: a psychological theory of motivation developed by Abraham Maslow in the 1940s and 1950s, according to which behavior in healthy human subjects is motivated by needs that progress up a pyramid from the physiological level at the base, to safety, love and belonging, esteem, and, self-actualization at the apex.

Holocaust: the genocide of European Jews and other marginalized groups by Nazi Germany; the word comes from the ancient Greek for "burnt whole," signifying a massive slaughter.

I Smile Back: a 2015 film directed by Adam Salky and produced by Egoli Tossell Film and Koppelman/Levien.

Kinsey reports: publications of the findings of the American biologist Alfred Charles Kinsey on human male sexuality (1948) and human female sexuality (1953).

Labor movement: a collective effort by workers and activists to obtain legal protections from governments and improved compensation and working conditions from employers.

Mad Men: a television series created by Matthew Reiner and produced by Lionsgate Television, set in the advertising industry of the 1960s, that ran from 2007 to 2015.

McCarthyism: the practice of accusing individuals of political disloyalty without respect for standards of evidence, named after Republican senator and subcommittee chair, Joseph McCarthy (1908–57). In the 1950s, McCarthy ordered aggressive investigations of suspected communists and held public hearings to accuse individuals in the government, military, media, and other sectors. Even though unsupported by the requisite evidence, the accusations ruined people's careers and generated widespread suspicion and fear.

National Federation of Business and Professional Women's Clubs: an American organization formed in 1919 to promote fair and productive policies and workplace conditions. Now called the Business and Professional Women's Foundation.

National Organization for Women (NOW): an American women's organization formed in 1966 by Betty Friedan and 48 other members over frustration at the lack of enforcement of antidiscrimination laws. Today the organization has 550 chapters in all states and the District of Columbia.

National Woman's Party: an American women's organization formed initially to fight for women's suffrage. The organization was disbanded in 1997.

National Women's Political Caucus: an organization founded in 1971 by Betty Friedan, Gloria Steinem, Bella Abzug, and others, to increase the presence of women in American politics and government and to influence policy.

The New School: formerly the New School for Social Research and the New School University, an American private research university founded in 1919 in New York City by progressive educators and divided into seven schools.

New York University: a private, nondenominational American research university founded in New York City in 1831, organized into more than 20 schools and with upward of a dozen academic programs abroad.

Oberlin College: a private, nondenominational American liberal arts college formed in 1833 in Oberlin, Ohio; the first US higher education institution to regularly enroll women and minority students.

Penis envy: in classical psychoanalytical theory as set out by Sigmund Freud, this is the desire for a penis—a desire Freud claimed was the cause of psychological problems and feelings of inferiority in girls and women.

Performativity (of gender): the enactment of culturally defined gender expectations through daily life that results in their embodiment, continually creating and reinforcing individual gender identity.

Popular Front: a coalition of leftist and center-left political parties formed in Europe and the United States during the 1930s to oppose fascism and promote social reform without requiring the destruction of capitalism.

Psychoanalysis: a therapeutic and theoretical approach to understanding the workings of the unconscious mind, founded by the Austrian neurologist Sigmund Freud in the late nineteenth century.

Psychotic episode: a period in which a person loses contact with normal reality through confused thinking, emotional disturbance, hallucinations, or delusions.

Second Wave feminism: the women's movement in the US and Europe from the late 1960s to the late 1980s.

Self-actualization: the achievement and continued exercise of individual abilities through sustained effort in education, training, and work, putting the self in relation to others and society.

Sex: a biological classification of organisms as female or male based on reproductive anatomy and functions; a group of organisms so classified; sexual activity. In Friedan's analysis, a sex role is a social role based on anatomical and physiological characteristics and the presumed personality traits dictated by them.

Sexuality: the characteristics and way of being of individuals in relation to sex; sexual attractiveness, potency, and expression.

Simple (nuclear) family: group consisting of a mother and father and their children, contrasting to other groups such as an extended family unit, containing grandparents or uncles and aunts as well as parents and children.

Smith College: a private, nondenominational American liberal arts college for women founded in 1871 in Northampton, Massachusetts. The largest of the Seven Sisters consortium of colleges, Smith College also provides graduate and certificate programs for women and men.

Sociology: the study of social behavior, social institutions, and the origins and organization of human society.

Third Wave feminism: a collection of women's movements and gender theories in the US and Europe from the late 1980s and early 1990s to the present.

Third Wave Foundation: a nonprofit organization founded in 1992 by Amy Richards and Rebecca Walker to promote young women's political involvement, leadership, and activism.

University of California at Berkeley: an American university in the University of California system, located in the city of Berkeley on the San Francisco Bay. Founded in 1868.

University of Southern California: a private nondenominational American research university founded in 1880 in Los Angeles.

Urban myth: an exaggerated account, spread by word of mouth—often with a shocking or disgusting element.

Women's Strike for Equality: a march through New York City on August 26, 1970, to celebrate the 50th anniversary of the women's suffrage amendment. The march was organized by Bella Abzug, Betty Friedan, and Gloria Steinem.

Women's Suffrage Amendment: the 19th amendment to the US constitution, passed in 1919 and ratified in 1920, which prohibits all states from denying women the right to vote.

World War I: the war fought between 1914 and 1918 in which Austria-Hungary, Germany, Turkey, and Bulgaria were defeated by Great Britain, France, Italy, Russia, Japan, the US, and other allies.

World War II: Global conflict between 1939 and 1945 that pitted the Axis Powers of Nazi Germany, Fascist Italy and Imperial Japan against the Allied nations including Britain, the United States and the Soviet Union.

Yale University: an American private Ivy League research university founded in 1701 in New Haven, Connecticut, to educate Congregationalist ministers and now divided into 12 schools.

PEOPLE MENTIONED IN THE TEXT

Bella Abzug (1920–88) was an American politician and the co-convener of the Women's Strike for Equality march in New York City in 1970. Abzug was a US Representative from New York from 1971 to 1976.

Margaret Atwood (b. 1939) is a Canadian writer, environmentalist, and businesswoman. She has written poetry, short stories, and novels including *The Handmaid's Tale* (1986), and is a cofounder of the Writers Trust of Canada.

Simone de Beauvoir (1908–86) was a French philosopher and feminist writer. She is best known for her critique of conventional gender beliefs and roles in *The Second Sex* (1949).

Bruno Bettelheim (1903–90) was an American psychologist born in Austria who was imprisoned in a concentration camp during World War II. Bettelheim is known for his work on education and child development.

Judith Butler (b. 1956) is an American scholar of gender, philosophy, and literary theory known for her analysis of concepts including gender and for her theories of gender performativity; she is best known for her 1990 book, *Gender Trouble*.

Michael Cunningham (b. 1952) is an American author of short stories, novels, and screenplays, and a creative writing instructor. He is best known for his 1998 novel, *The Hours*.

Helene Deutsch (1884–1982) was an American psychoanalyst born in Austrian Poland. Deutsch was analyzed by and worked with Sigmund Freud, and became the first psychoanalyst to specialize in women. Deutsch's work was shaped by her admiration for and identification with her father, as well as Freud, and her dislike of her mother and disparagement of her superficiality and discontent.

Marlene Dietrich (1901–92) was a German-born American singer and actress known for her sultry voice and for playing the role of alluring women in films such as *The Blue Angel* (1930).

Dwight David Eisenhower (1890–1969) was an American general during World War II, and the 34th president of the United States between 1953 and 1961.

Friedrich Engels (1820–95) was a German philosopher and social theorist who coauthored *The Communist Manifesto* (1848) with Karl Marx, and collaborated with Marx on many other works.

Erik Erikson (1902–94) was a German American psychoanalyst and developmental psychologist known for his theories on psychosocial development and identity formation, and the concept of "identity crisis." Erikson never finished a university degree, but he earned both a Montessori diploma and a diploma from the Vienna Psychoanalytic Institute, where Anna Freud trained him.

Marynia Farnham (1900–79) was an American psychiatrist and vocal proponent of women's return to the home and childbearing after World War II. Together with Ferdinand Lundberg, she wrote *Modern Woman: The Lost Sex* (1947), which argued that the social disorganization caused by women's competition with men in the workplace caused neuroses that threatened to pass into the next generation.

Jo Freeman (b. 1945) is an American feminist writer, civil rights and peace activist, and lawyer who was one of the leaders of the women's movement in the late 1960s and 1970s.

Sigmund Freud (1856–1939) was an Austrian physician who founded the field of psychoanalysis. Freud is known for his theories about the origins of hysteria and other psychological disorders in childhood psychosexual traumas and unresolved conflicts.

Greta Garbo (1905–90) was a reclusive Swedish-born American actress known for films including *Queen Christina* (1933) and *Camille* (1936).

Charlotte Perkins Gilman (1860–1935) was an American writer, commercial artist, feminist, and social theorist and reformer. She is best known for the short story "The Yellow Wall-Paper" (1892) which describes the damaging physical and mental effects of women's enforced domesticity.

Adolf Hitler (1889–1945) was a German politician and dictator and leader of the right-wing Nazi party. He ruled Germany from 1933 to 1945, including the period during World War II. As head of the German state, he was responsible for attempting genocide by killing 6,000,000 Jewish people and political prisoners in the concentration camps.

bell hooks (b. 1952 Gloria Jean Watkins) is an American social activist, cultural critic, and feminist author known for her work on systems of gender, race, and class oppression.

Daniel Horowitz (b. 1938) is an American professor emeritus of American Studies at Smith College who specializes in twentieth-century consumer culture and social criticism in the US, including feminism and union activism during the Cold War. He has written critical analyses of Betty Friedan's life and publications.

John Fitzgerald Kennedy (1917–63) was an American politician. He was a US representative from Massachusetts from 1947 to 1953, a US senator from 1953 to 1960, and the 35th president of the US from 1961 to 1963.

Alfred Charles Kinsey (1894–1956) was an American biologist known for his studies of human sexual behavior, published as *Sexual Behavior in the Human Male* (1948) and *Sexual Behavior in the Human Female* (1953).

Viola Klein (1908–73) was a British sociologist from Austria known for demonstrating social changes through quantitative evidence, including shifts in women's roles after the Industrial Revolution.

Mirra Komarovsky (1905–99) was a Russian-born American sociologist of gender who is known for the concept of "cultural lag," describing the delayed shifts in gender roles compared to technological and social changes. In 1973 she became the second woman president of the America Sociological Association.

Ferdinand Lundberg (1902–95) was an American journalist, biographer, and social critic. Together with Marynia Farnham, he wrote *Modern Woman: The Lost Sex* (1947), which argued that the social disorganization caused by women's competition with men in the workplace caused neuroses that threatened to pass into the next generation.

Karl Marx (1818–83) was a German philosopher, economic historian, and revolutionary social theorist who argued that class struggle would eventually lead to a classless communist society. He wrote *Das Kapital* (1867–94) and coauthored *The Communist Manifesto* (1848) with Friedrich Engels.

Abraham Harold Maslow (1908–70) was an American psychologist trained in experimental-behavioral psychology who is known for his theory of the "hierarchy of needs," according to which needs are fulfilled in order from survival needs to the highest human need of self-actualization.

Margaret Mead (1901–78) was an American anthropologist and public figure who conducted research in Melanesia and the South Pacific on gender roles, sexuality, childrearing, and adolescence.

Marilyn Monroe (1926–62) was an American actress known for films including *Some Like It Hot* (1959) and *The Misfits* (1961), her performances for soldiers in Korea, and for her early death.

Lucretia Coffin Mott (1793–1880) was an American abolitionist, feminist, and social reformer who co-convened the first convention for women's rights in the US, held in 1848.

Alva Myrdal (1902–86) was a Swedish diplomat and sociologist who wrote about women's domestic and professional roles in the 1950s. She was awarded the Nobel Peace Prize in 1982 for her work on nuclear disarmament.

Kate O'Beirne (b. 1949) is an American conservative print and television journalist and political commentator, and author of *Women Who Make the World Worse: and How Their Radical Feminist Assault Is Ruining Our Schools, Families, Military, and Sports* (2005).

Vance Packard (1914–96) was an American writer, journalist, and social critic. He is best known for *The Hidden Persuaders* (1957), which explores the use of psychological techniques in advertising to manipulate perceptions and create consumer desire.

Camille Paglia (b. 1947) is an American social critic and professor of humanities and media studies who analyzes visual culture, music, film, and sexuality and gender from a feminist perspective.

Talcott Parsons (1902–79) was an American sociologist known for applying structural-functionalism to the study of social systems and for his collaboration and influence across many academic disciplines.

Debbie Reynolds (b. 1932) is an American singer, dancer, cabaret performer, businesswoman, and film, stage, and television actress. The film *Singin' in the Rain* (1952) launched her career.

Amy Richards (b. 1970) is an American writer and social activist who coauthored the foundational Third Wave feminist text *Manifesta: Young Women, Feminism, and the Future* (2000). Richards cofounded the Third Wave Foundation and has written about twenty-first-century motherhood from a Third Wave feminist perspective.

Ernestine Rose (1810–92) was a Polish-born abolitionist, atheist feminist, activist, and public lecturer. She spoke out against oppression beginning in adolescence when she successfully resisted an arranged marriage, and continued throughout a life spent in northern Europe, the United Kingdom, and the United States.

Olive Schreiner (1855–1920) was a South African author and activist who spent much of her adult life in the United Kingdom and Europe. She advocated on behalf of women and oppressed groups in South Africa and elsewhere and is best known for her novel *The Story of an African Farm* (1883).

Elizabeth Cady Stanton (1815–1902) was an American feminist and social reformer. She co-convened and wrote the *Declaration of Sentiments* for the first women's rights convention in the United States, held in 1848.

Gloria Steinem (b. 1934) is an American feminist writer, activist, and founding editor of *Ms.* magazine. She was a main voice of the American feminist movement of the late 1960s and 1970s.

Lucy Stone (1818–93) was an American feminist and social reformer who founded the American Woman Suffrage Association in 1869. Stone helped organize the first National Women's Rights Convention in 1850.

Rebecca Walker (b. 1969) is a *Black, White, and Jewish* (the title of her 2001 memoir) American writer and social activist who has played a central role in defining and launching Third Wave feminism. She cofounded the Third Wave Foundation in 1992.

Alan Wolfe (b. 1942) is an American political scientist and sociologist who teaches at Boston College and directs its Boisi Center for Religion and American Public Life.

Virginia Woolf (1882–1941) was a leading English modernist novelist, essayist, and social critic. She is best known for the novels *Mrs. Dalloway* (1925) and *To the Lighthouse* (1927), and the book-length essay, *A Room of One's Own* (1929).

WORKS CITED

WORKS CITED

Atwood, Margaret. *The Handmaid's Tale*. Boston, MA: Houghton, Mifflin & Co., 1986.

Barclay, Marion S., and Frances Champion. *Teen Guide to Homemaking*. New York: McGraw-Hill, 1967.

Baumgardner, Jennifer, and Amy Richards. *Manifesta: Young Women, Feminism, and the Future.* New York: Farrar, Straus, and Giroux, 2000.

de Beauvoir, Simone. *The Second Sex*. Translated by H. M. Parshley. New York: Vintage, 1953.

— — —. *The Coming of Age*. Translated by Patrick O'Brian. New York: Putnam, 1972.

Bowlby, Rachel. *Still Crazy After All These Years: Women, Writing, and Psychoanalysis*. New York: Routledge, 1992.

Butler, Judith. *Gender Trouble: Feminism and the Subversion of Identity*. New York: Routledge, 1990.

— — —. *Bodies that Matter: On the Discursive Limits of "Sex."* New York: Routledge, 1993.

Collins, Gail. Introduction to *The Feminine Mystique*, by Betty Friedan. New York: W. W. Norton & Company, 2013.

Coontz, Stephanie. *A Strange Stirring:* The Feminine Mystique *and American Women at the Dawn of the 1960s*. New York: Basic Books, 2011.

Cunningham, Michael. *The Hours*. New York: Farrar, Straus, and Giroux, 1998.

Deutsch, Helene. *The Psychology of Women: A Psychoanalytic Interpretation*. 2 vols. Boston: Allyn & Bacon, 1943, 1945.

Dobrin, Lise M., and Ira Bashkow. "'Arapesh Warfare': Reo Fortune's veiled critique of Margaret Mead's *Sex and Temperament*." *American Anthropologist* 112, no. 3 (2010): 370–83.

Ehrenreich, Barbara. *Bright-Sided: How Positive Thinking is Undermining America*. New York: Picador, 2009.

Farnham, Marynia, and Ferdinand Lundberg. *Modern Woman: The Lost Sex*. New York: Harper & Brothers, 1947.

Frech, Adrianne, and Sarah Damaske. "The Relationships between Mothers' Work Pathways and Physical and Mental Health." *Journal of Health and Social Behavior* 53, no. 4 (2012): 396–412.

Friedan, Betty. *The Second Stage*. New York: Simon & Schuster, 1981.

———. *Beyond Gender: The New Politics of Work and Family*. Washington, DC: Woodrow Wilson Center Press, 1997.

———. *"It Changed My Life": Writings on the Women's Movement*. Cambridge, MA: Harvard University Press, 1998.

———. *Life So Far: A Memoir*. New York: Simon & Schuster, 2000.

———. *The Fountain of Age*. New York: Simon & Schuster, 2006.

———. *The Feminine Mystique*. 50th Anniversary Edition. Introduction by Gail Collins. New York: W. W. Norton & Company, 2013.

Gilman, Charlotte Perkins. "The Yellow Wall-Paper." *New England Magazine* 11, no. 5 (1892): 647–56.

Heise, Lori L. "Violence, Sexuality, and Women's Lives." In *The Gender/Sexuality Reader*, edited by Roger N. Lancaster and Micaela di Leonardo, 411–33. New York: Routledge, 1997.

hooks, bell. *Ain't I a Woman? Black Women and Feminism*. Boston, MA: South End Press, 1981.

———. *Feminist Theory from Margin to Center*. Boston, MA: South End Press, 1984.

———. *We Real Cool: Black Men and Masculinity*. New York: Routledge, 2004.

Horowitz, Daniel. *Betty Friedan and the Making of* The Feminine Mystique*: The American Left, the Cold War, and Modern Feminism*. Amherst: University of Massachusetts Press, 2000.

Jones, James H. *Alfred C. Kinsey: A Public/Private Life.* New York: W. W. Norton, 1997.

Kinsey, Alfred Charles, Wardell B. Pomeroy, and Clyde E. Martin. *Sexual Behavior in the Human Male*. Bloomington: Indiana University Press, 1949.

Kinsey, Alfred Charles, Wardell B. Pomeroy, Clyde E. Martin, and Paul H. Gebhard. *Sexual Behavior in the Human Female*. Bloomington: Indiana University Press, 1953.

Komarovsky, Mirra. *Women in the Modern World: Their Education and Their Dilemmas*. Boston, MA: Little, Brown & Co., 1953.

Lucas-Thompson, Rachel G., Wendy A. Goldberg, and JoAnn Prause. "Maternal Work Early in the Lives of Children and its Distal Associations with Achievement and Behavior Problems: a Meta-Analysis." *Psychological Bulletin* 136, no. 6 (2010): 915–42.

Lythcott-Haims, Julie. *How to Raise an Adult: Break Free of the Overparenting Trap and Prepare Your Kids for Success*. New York: Henry Holt & Co., 2015.

Martin, Emily. *The Woman in the Body: A Cultural Analysis of Reproduction*. Boston, MA: Beacon Press, 1987.

Mead, Margaret. *Sex and Temperament in Three Primitive Societies*. New York: William Morrow, 1935.

———. *Male and Female: A Study of the Sexes in a Changing World*. New York: William Morrow, 1949.

Meyerowitz, Joanne, ed. *Not June Cleaver: Women and Gender in Postwar America, 1945–1960*. Philadelphia: Temple University Press, 1994.

Myrdal, Alva, and Viola Klein. *Woman's Two Roles: Home and Work*. London: Routledge & Kegan Paul, 1956.

O'Beirne, Kate. *Women Who Made the World Worse: And How Their Radical Feminist Assault Is Ruining Our Schools, Families, Military, and Sports.* New York: Sentinel, 2005.

Oliver, Susan. *Betty Friedan: The Personal Is Political*. New York: Pearson Longman, 2008.

Packard, Vance. *The Hidden Persuaders*. Philadelphia: David McKay Company, 1957.

Paglia, Camille. "The Modern Campus Cannot Comprehend Evil." *Time*, September 29, 2014. Accessed October 31, 2015. http://time.com/3444749/camille-paglia-the-modern-campus-cannot-comprehend-evil/.

Parsons, Talcott. *Essays in Sociological Theory*. New York: Free Press, 1958.

Pollak, Richard. *The Creation of Dr. B.: A Biography of Bruno Bettelheim*. New York: Simon & Schuster, 1997.

Public Broadcasting Service. "Betty Friedan and *The Feminine Mystique*." Accessed October 31, 2015. http://www.pbs.org/fmc/segments/progseg11.htm.

Quindlen, Anna. "Afterword." In *The Feminine Mystique*, by Betty Friedan, 477–82. New York: W. W. Norton & Company, 2013.

Quine, Maria Sophia. *Population Politics in Twentieth-Century Europe: Fascist Dictatorships and Liberal Democracies*. London: Routledge, 1996.

Richards, Amy. *Opting In: Having a Child without Losing Yourself*. New York: Farrar, Straus, and Giroux, 2008.

Scheussler, Jennifer. "Criticisms of a Classic Unbound." *New York Times*, February 18, 2013.

Schreiner, Olive. *Women and Labor*. New York: Frederick A. Stokes, 1911.

Solnit, Rebecca. "The Mother of All Questions." *Harper's* 331, no. 1985 (2015): 5–7.

Spencer, Steven J., Claude M. Steele, and Diane M. Quinn. "Stereotype Threat and Women's Math Performance." *Journal of Experimental Social Psychology* 35 (1999): 4–28.

Stuart-Macadam, Patricia, and Katherine Dettwyler, eds. *Breastfeeding: Biocultural Perspectives*. New York: Aldine de Gruyter, 1995.

United States Department of Labor. "Books That Shaped Work in America." Accessed December 23, 2015. http://www.dol.gov/100/books-shaped-work/initiative.htm.

Vonnegut, Kurt. *Bagombo Snuff Box: Uncollected Short Fiction*. New York: G. P. Putnam's Sons, 1999.

Walker, Rebecca. *Black, White, and Jewish: Autobiography of a Shifting Self*. New York: Riverhead Books, 2001.

———, ed. *To Be Real: Telling the Truth and Changing the Face of Feminism*. New York: Anchor Books, 1995.

Wolfe, Alan. "The Mystique of Betty Friedan." *The Atlantic* 284, no. 3 (1999): 98–105.

Woolf, Virginia. *Mrs. Dalloway*. London: Hogarth Press, 1925.

———. *To the Lighthouse*. London: Hogarth Press, 1927.

———. *A Room of One's Own* and *Three Guineas*. Oxford: Oxford University Press, 2015.

THE MACAT LIBRARY
BY DISCIPLINE

AFRICANA STUDIES

Chinua Achebe's *An Image of Africa: Racism in Conrad's Heart of Darkness*
W. E. B. Du Bois's *The Souls of Black Folk*
Zora Neale Huston's *Characteristics of Negro Expression*
Martin Luther King Jr's *Why We Can't Wait*
Toni Morrison's *Playing in the Dark: Whiteness in the American Literary Imagination*

ANTHROPOLOGY

Arjun Appadurai's *Modernity at Large: Cultural Dimensions of Globalisation*
Philippe Ariès's *Centuries of Childhood*
Franz Boas's *Race, Language and Culture*
Kim Chan & Renée Mauborgne's *Blue Ocean Strategy*
Jared Diamond's *Guns, Germs & Steel: the Fate of Human Societies*
Jared Diamond's *Collapse: How Societies Choose to Fail or Survive*
E. E. Evans-Pritchard's *Witchcraft, Oracles and Magic Among the Azande*
James Ferguson's *The Anti-Politics Machine*
Clifford Geertz's *The Interpretation of Cultures*
David Graeber's *Debt: the First 5000 Years*
Karen Ho's *Liquidated: An Ethnography of Wall Street*
Geert Hofstede's *Culture's Consequences: Comparing Values, Behaviors, Institutes and Organizations across Nations*
Claude Lévi-Strauss's *Structural Anthropology*
Jay Macleod's *Ain't No Makin' It: Aspirations and Attainment in a Low-Income Neighborhood*
Saba Mahmood's *The Politics of Piety: The Islamic Revival and the Feminist Subjec*t
Marcel Mauss's *The Gift*

BUSINESS

Jean Lave & Etienne Wenger's *Situated Learning*
Theodore Levitt's *Marketing Myopia*
Burton G. Malkiel's *A Random Walk Down Wall Street*
Douglas McGregor's *The Human Side of Enterprise*
Michael Porter's *Competitive Strategy: Creating and Sustaining Superior Performance*
John Kotter's *Leading Change*
C. K. Prahalad & Gary Hamel's *The Core Competence of the Corporation*

CRIMINOLOGY

Michelle Alexander's *The New Jim Crow: Mass Incarceration in the Age of Colorblindness*
Michael R. Gottfredson & Travis Hirschi's *A General Theory of Crime*
Richard Herrnstein & Charles A. Murray's *The Bell Curve: Intelligence and Class Structure in American Life*
Elizabeth Loftus's *Eyewitness Testimony*
Jay Macleod's *Ain't No Makin' It: Aspirations and Attainment in a Low-Income Neighborhood*
Philip Zimbardo's *The Lucifer Effect*

ECONOMICS

Janet Abu-Lughod's *Before European Hegemony*
Ha-Joon Chang's *Kicking Away the Ladder*
David Brion Davis's *The Problem of Slavery in the Age of Revolution*
Milton Friedman's *The Role of Monetary Policy*
Milton Friedman's *Capitalism and Freedom*
David Graeber's *Debt: the First 5000 Years*
Friedrich Hayek's *The Road to Serfdom*
Karen Ho's *Liquidated: An Ethnography of Wall Street*

John Maynard Keynes's *The General Theory of Employment, Interest and Money*
Charles P. Kindleberger's *Manias, Panics and Crashes*
Robert Lucas's *Why Doesn't Capital Flow from Rich to Poor Countries?*
Burton G. Malkiel's *A Random Walk Down Wall Street*
Thomas Robert Malthus's *An Essay on the Principle of Population*
Karl Marx's *Capital*
Thomas Piketty's *Capital in the Twenty-First Century*
Amartya Sen's *Development as Freedom*
Adam Smith's *The Wealth of Nations*
Nassim Nicholas Taleb's *The Black Swan: The Impact of the Highly Improbable*
Amos Tversky's & Daniel Kahneman's *Judgment under Uncertainty: Heuristics and Biases*
Mahbub Ul Haq's *Reflections on Human Development*
Max Weber's *The Protestant Ethic and the Spirit of Capitalism*

FEMINISM AND GENDER STUDIES

Judith Butler's *Gender Trouble*
Simone De Beauvoir's *The Second Sex*
Michel Foucault's *History of Sexuality*
Betty Friedan's *The Feminine Mystique*
Saba Mahmood's *The Politics of Piety: The Islamic Revival and the Feminist Subject*
Joan Wallach Scott's *Gender and the Politics of History*
Mary Wollstonecraft's *A Vindication of the Rights of Woman*
Virginia Woolf's *A Room of One's Own*

GEOGRAPHY

The Brundtland Report's *Our Common Future*
Rachel Carson's *Silent Spring*
Charles Darwin's *On the Origin of Species*
James Ferguson's *The Anti-Politics Machine*
Jane Jacobs's *The Death and Life of Great American Cities*
James Lovelock's *Gaia: A New Look at Life on Earth*
Amartya Sen's *Development as Freedom*
Mathis Wackernagel & William Rees's *Our Ecological Footprint*

HISTORY

Janet Abu-Lughod's *Before European Hegemony*
Benedict Anderson's *Imagined Communities*
Bernard Bailyn's *The Ideological Origins of the American Revolution*
Hanna Batatu's *The Old Social Classes And The Revolutionary Movements Of Iraq*
Christopher Browning's *Ordinary Men: Reserve Police Batallion 101 and the Final Solution in Poland*
Edmund Burke's *Reflections on the Revolution in France*
William Cronon's *Nature's Metropolis: Chicago And The Great West*
Alfred W. Crosby's *The Columbian Exchange*
Hamid Dabashi's *Iran: A People Interrupted*
David Brion Davis's *The Problem of Slavery in the Age of Revolution*
Nathalie Zemon Davis's *The Return of Martin Guerre*
Jared Diamond's *Guns, Germs & Steel: the Fate of Human Societies*
Frank Dikotter's *Mao's Great Famine*
John W Dower's *War Without Mercy: Race And Power In The Pacific War*
W. E. B. Du Bois's *The Souls of Black Folk*
Richard J. Evans's *In Defence of History*
Lucien Febvre's *The Problem of Unbelief in the 16th Century*
Sheila Fitzpatrick's *Everyday Stalinism*

Eric Foner's *Reconstruction: America's Unfinished Revolution, 1863-1877*
Michel Foucault's *Discipline and Punish*
Michel Foucault's *History of Sexuality*
Francis Fukuyama's *The End of History and the Last Man*
John Lewis Gaddis's *We Now Know: Rethinking Cold War History*
Ernest Gellner's *Nations and Nationalism*
Eugene Genovese's *Roll, Jordan, Roll: The World the Slaves Made*
Carlo Ginzburg's *The Night Battles*
Daniel Goldhagen's *Hitler's Willing Executioners*
Jack Goldstone's *Revolution and Rebellion in the Early Modern World*
Antonio Gramsci's *The Prison Notebooks*
Alexander Hamilton, John Jay & James Madison's *The Federalist Papers*
Christopher Hill's *The World Turned Upside Down*
Carole Hillenbrand's *The Crusades: Islamic Perspectives*
Thomas Hobbes's *Leviathan*
Eric Hobsbawm's *The Age Of Revolution*
John A. Hobson's *Imperialism: A Study*
Albert Hourani's *History of the Arab Peoples*
Samuel P. Huntington's *The Clash of Civilizations and the Remaking of World Order*
C. L. R. James's *The Black Jacobins*
Tony Judt's *Postwar: A History of Europe Since 1945*
Ernst Kantorowicz's *The King's Two Bodies: A Study in Medieval Political Theology*
Paul Kennedy's *The Rise and Fall of the Great Powers*
Ian Kershaw's *The "Hitler Myth": Image and Reality in the Third Reich*
John Maynard Keynes's *The General Theory of Employment, Interest and Money*
Charles P. Kindleberger's *Manias, Panics and Crashes*
Martin Luther King Jr's *Why We Can't Wait*
Henry Kissinger's *World Order: Reflections on the Character of Nations and the Course of History*
Thomas Kuhn's *The Structure of Scientific Revolutions*
Georges Lefebvre's *The Coming of the French Revolution*
John Locke's *Two Treatises of Government*
Niccolò Machiavelli's *The Prince*
Thomas Robert Malthus's *An Essay on the Principle of Population*
Mahmood Mamdani's *Citizen and Subject: Contemporary Africa And The Legacy Of Late Colonialism*
Karl Marx's *Capital*
Stanley Milgram's *Obedience to Authority*
John Stuart Mill's *On Liberty*
Thomas Paine's *Common Sense*
Thomas Paine's *Rights of Man*
Geoffrey Parker's *Global Crisis: War, Climate Change and Catastrophe in the Seventeenth Century*
Jonathan Riley-Smith's *The First Crusade and the Idea of Crusading*
Jean-Jacques Rousseau's *The Social Contract*
Joan Wallach Scott's *Gender and the Politics of History*
Theda Skocpol's *States and Social Revolutions*
Adam Smith's *The Wealth of Nations*
Timothy Snyder's *Bloodlands: Europe Between Hitler and Stalin*
Sun Tzu's *The Art of War*
Keith Thomas's *Religion and the Decline of Magic*
Thucydides's *The History of the Peloponnesian War*
Frederick Jackson Turner's *The Significance of the Frontier in American History*
Odd Arne Westad's *The Global Cold War: Third World Interventions And The Making Of Our Times*

LITERATURE

Chinua Achebe's *An Image of Africa: Racism in Conrad's Heart of Darkness*
Roland Barthes's *Mythologies*
Homi K. Bhabha's *The Location of Culture*
Judith Butler's *Gender Trouble*
Simone De Beauvoir's *The Second Sex*
Ferdinand De Saussure's *Course in General Linguistics*
T. S. Eliot's *The Sacred Wood: Essays on Poetry and Criticism*
Zora Neale Huston's *Characteristics of Negro Expression*
Toni Morrison's *Playing in the Dark: Whiteness in the American Literary Imagination*
Edward Said's *Orientalism*
Gayatri Chakravorty Spivak's *Can the Subaltern Speak?*
Mary Wollstonecraft's *A Vindication of the Rights of Women*
Virginia Woolf's *A Room of One's Own*

PHILOSOPHY

Elizabeth Anscombe's *Modern Moral Philosophy*
Hannah Arendt's *The Human Condition*
Aristotle's *Metaphysics*
Aristotle's *Nicomachean Ethics*
Edmund Gettier's *Is Justified True Belief Knowledge?*
Georg Wilhelm Friedrich Hegel's *Phenomenology of Spirit*
David Hume's *Dialogues Concerning Natural Religion*
David Hume's *The Enquiry for Human Understanding*
Immanuel Kant's *Religion within the Boundaries of Mere Reason*
Immanuel Kant's *Critique of Pure Reason*
Søren Kierkegaard's *The Sickness Unto Death*
Søren Kierkegaard's *Fear and Trembling*
C. S. Lewis's *The Abolition of Man*
Alasdair MacIntyre's *After Virtue*
Marcus Aurelius's *Meditations*
Friedrich Nietzsche's *On the Genealogy of Morality*
Friedrich Nietzsche's *Beyond Good and Evil*
Plato's *Republic*
Plato's *Symposium*
Jean-Jacques Rousseau's *The Social Contract*
Gilbert Ryle's *The Concept of Mind*
Baruch Spinoza's *Ethics*
Sun Tzu's *The Art of War*
Ludwig Wittgenstein's *Philosophical Investigations*

POLITICS

Benedict Anderson's *Imagined Communities*
Aristotle's *Politics*
Bernard Bailyn's *The Ideological Origins of the American Revolution*
Edmund Burke's *Reflections on the Revolution in France*
John C. Calhoun's *A Disquisition on Government*
Ha-Joon Chang's *Kicking Away the Ladder*
Hamid Dabashi's *Iran: A People Interrupted*
Hamid Dabashi's *Theology of Discontent: The Ideological Foundation of the Islamic Revolution in Iran*
Robert Dahl's *Democracy and its Critics*
Robert Dahl's *Who Governs?*
David Brion Davis's *The Problem of Slavery in the Age of Revolution*

Alexis De Tocqueville's *Democracy in America*
James Ferguson's *The Anti-Politics Machine*
Frank Dikotter's *Mao's Great Famine*
Sheila Fitzpatrick's *Everyday Stalinism*
Eric Foner's *Reconstruction: America's Unfinished Revolution, 1863-1877*
Milton Friedman's *Capitalism and Freedom*
Francis Fukuyama's *The End of History and the Last Man*
John Lewis Gaddis's *We Now Know: Rethinking Cold War History*
Ernest Gellner's *Nations and Nationalism*
David Graeber's *Debt: the First 5000 Years*
Antonio Gramsci's *The Prison Notebooks*
Alexander Hamilton, John Jay & James Madison's *The Federalist Papers*
Friedrich Hayek's *The Road to Serfdom*
Christopher Hill's *The World Turned Upside Down*
Thomas Hobbes's *Leviathan*
John A. Hobson's *Imperialism: A Study*
Samuel P. Huntington's *The Clash of Civilizations and the Remaking of World Order*
Tony Judt's *Postwar: A History of Europe Since 1945*
David C. Kang's *China Rising: Peace, Power and Order in East Asia*
Paul Kennedy's *The Rise and Fall of Great Powers*
Robert Keohane's *After Hegemony*
Martin Luther King Jr.'s *Why We Can't Wait*
Henry Kissinger's *World Order: Reflections on the Character of Nations and the Course of History*
John Locke's *Two Treatises of Government*
Niccolò Machiavelli's *The Prince*
Thomas Robert Malthus's *An Essay on the Principle of Population*
Mahmood Mamdani's *Citizen and Subject: Contemporary Africa And The Legacy Of Late Colonialism*
Karl Marx's *Capital*
John Stuart Mill's *On Liberty*
John Stuart Mill's *Utilitarianism*
Hans Morgenthau's *Politics Among Nations*
Thomas Paine's *Common Sense*
Thomas Paine's *Rights of Man*
Thomas Piketty's *Capital in the Twenty-First Century*
Robert D. Putman's *Bowling Alone*
John Rawls's *Theory of Justice*
Jean-Jacques Rousseau's *The Social Contract*
Theda Skocpol's *States and Social Revolutions*
Adam Smith's *The Wealth of Nations*
Sun Tzu's *The Art of War*
Henry David Thoreau's *Civil Disobedience*
Thucydides's *The History of the Peloponnesian War*
Kenneth Waltz's *Theory of International Politics*
Max Weber's *Politics as a Vocation*
Odd Arne Westad's *The Global Cold War: Third World Interventions And The Making Of Our Times*

POSTCOLONIAL STUDIES

Roland Barthes's *Mythologies*
Frantz Fanon's *Black Skin, White Masks*
Homi K. Bhabha's *The Location of Culture*
Gustavo Gutiérrez's *A Theology of Liberation*
Edward Said's *Orientalism*
Gayatri Chakravorty Spivak's *Can the Subaltern Speak?*

PSYCHOLOGY

Gordon Allport's *The Nature of Prejudice*
Alan Baddeley & Graham Hitch's *Aggression: A Social Learning Analysis*
Albert Bandura's *Aggression: A Social Learning Analysis*
Leon Festinger's *A Theory of Cognitive Dissonance*
Sigmund Freud's *The Interpretation of Dreams*
Betty Friedan's *The Feminine Mystique*
Michael R. Gottfredson & Travis Hirschi's *A General Theory of Crime*
Eric Hoffer's *The True Believer: Thoughts on the Nature of Mass Movements*
William James's *Principles of Psychology*
Elizabeth Loftus's *Eyewitness Testimony*
A. H. Maslow's *A Theory of Human Motivation*
Stanley Milgram's *Obedience to Authority*
Steven Pinker's *The Better Angels of Our Nature*
Oliver Sacks's *The Man Who Mistook His Wife For a Hat*
Richard Thaler & Cass Sunstein's *Nudge: Improving Decisions About Health, Wealth and Happiness*
Amos Tversky's *Judgment under Uncertainty: Heuristics and Biases*
Philip Zimbardo's *The Lucifer Effect*

SCIENCE

Rachel Carson's *Silent Spring*
William Cronon's *Nature's Metropolis: Chicago And The Great West*
Alfred W. Crosby's *The Columbian Exchange*
Charles Darwin's *On the Origin of Species*
Richard Dawkin's *The Selfish Gene*
Thomas Kuhn's *The Structure of Scientific Revolutions*
Geoffrey Parker's *Global Crisis: War, Climate Change and Catastrophe in the Seventeenth Century*
Mathis Wackernagel & William Rees's *Our Ecological Footprint*

SOCIOLOGY

Michelle Alexander's *The New Jim Crow: Mass Incarceration in the Age of Colorblindness*
Gordon Allport's *The Nature of Prejudice*
Albert Bandura's *Aggression: A Social Learning Analysis*
Hanna Batatu's *The Old Social Classes And The Revolutionary Movements Of Iraq*
Ha-Joon Chang's *Kicking Away the Ladder*
W. E. B. Du Bois's *The Souls of Black Folk*
Émile Durkheim's *On Suicide*
Frantz Fanon's *Black Skin, White Masks*
Frantz Fanon's *The Wretched of the Earth*
Eric Foner's *Reconstruction: America's Unfinished Revolution, 1863-1877*
Eugene Genovese's *Roll, Jordan, Roll: The World the Slaves Made*
Jack Goldstone's *Revolution and Rebellion in the Early Modern World*
Antonio Gramsci's *The Prison Notebooks*
Richard Herrnstein & Charles A Murray's *The Bell Curve: Intelligence and Class Structure in American Life*
Eric Hoffer's *The True Believer: Thoughts on the Nature of Mass Movements*
Jane Jacobs's *The Death and Life of Great American Cities*
Robert Lucas's *Why Doesn't Capital Flow from Rich to Poor Countries?*
Jay Macleod's *Ain't No Makin' It: Aspirations and Attainment in a Low Income Neighborhood*
Elaine May's *Homeward Bound: American Families in the Cold War Era*
Douglas McGregor's *The Human Side of Enterprise*
C. Wright Mills's *The Sociological Imagination*

Thomas Piketty's *Capital in the Twenty-First Century*
Robert D. Putman's *Bowling Alone*
David Riesman's *The Lonely Crowd: A Study of the Changing American Character*
Edward Said's *Orientalism*
Joan Wallach Scott's *Gender and the Politics of History*
Theda Skocpol's *States and Social Revolutions*
Max Weber's *The Protestant Ethic and the Spirit of Capitalism*

THEOLOGY

Augustine's *Confessions*
Benedict's *Rule of St Benedict*
Gustavo Gutiérrez's *A Theology of Liberation*
Carole Hillenbrand's *The Crusades: Islamic Perspectives*
David Hume's *Dialogues Concerning Natural Religion*
Immanuel Kant's *Religion within the Boundaries of Mere Reason*
Ernst Kantorowicz's *The King's Two Bodies: A Study in Medieval Political Theology*
Søren Kierkegaard's *The Sickness Unto Death*
C. S. Lewis's *The Abolition of Man*
Saba Mahmood's *The Politics of Piety: The Islamic Revival and the Feminist Subjec*t
Baruch Spinoza's *Ethics*
Keith Thomas's *Religion and the Decline of Magic*

COMING SOON

Chris Argyris's *The Individual and the Organisation*
Seyla Benhabib's *The Rights of Others*
Walter Benjamin's *The Work Of Art in the Age of Mechanical Reproduction*
John Berger's *Ways of Seeing*
Pierre Bourdieu's *Outline of a Theory of Practice*
Mary Douglas's *Purity and Danger*
Roland Dworkin's *Taking Rights Seriously*
James G. March's *Exploration and Exploitation in Organisational Learning*
Ikujiro Nonaka's *A Dynamic Theory of Organizational Knowledge Creation*
Griselda Pollock's *Vision and Difference*
Amartya Sen's *Inequality Re-Examined*
Susan Sontag's *On Photography*
Yasser Tabbaa's *The Transformation of Islamic Art*
Ludwig von Mises's *Theory of Money and Credit*

Macat Disciplines

Access the greatest ideas and thinkers across entire disciplines, including

FEMINISM, GENDER AND QUEER STUDIES

Simone De Beauvoir's
The Second Sex

Michel Foucault's
History of Sexuality

Betty Friedan's
The Feminine Mystique

Saba Mahmood's
*The Politics of Piety:
The Islamic Revival and
the Feminist Subject*

Joan Wallach Scott's
*Gender and the
Politics of History*

Mary Wollstonecraft's
*A Vindication of the
Rights of Woman*

Virginia Woolf's
A Room of One's Own

Judith Butler's
Gender Trouble

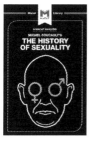

Macat analyses are available from all good bookshops and libraries.

Access hundreds of analyses through one, multimedia tool.
Join free for one month **library.macat.com**

Macat Disciplines

Access the greatest ideas and thinkers across entire disciplines, including

INEQUALITY

Ha-Joon Chang's, *Kicking Away the Ladder*

David Graeber's, *Debt: The First 5000 Years*

Robert E. Lucas's, *Why Doesn't Capital Flow from Rich To Poor Countries?*

Thomas Piketty's, *Capital in the Twenty-First Century*

Amartya Sen's, *Inequality Re-Examined*

Mahbub Ul Haq's, *Reflections on Human Development*

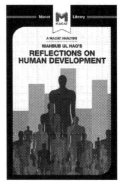

Macat analyses are available from all good bookshops and libraries.

Access hundreds of analyses through one, multimedia tool.
Join free for one month **library.macat.com**

Macat Disciplines

Access the greatest ideas and thinkers across entire disciplines, including

CRIMINOLOGY

Michelle Alexander's
*The New Jim Crow:
Mass Incarceration in the
Age of Colorblindness*

**Michael R. Gottfredson
& Travis Hirschi's**
A General Theory of Crime

Elizabeth Loftus's
Eyewitness Testimony

**Richard Herrnstein
& Charles A. Murray's**
*The Bell Curve: Intelligence and
Class Structure in American Life*

Jay Macleod's
*Ain't No Makin' It:
Aspirations and Attainment in a
Low-Income Neighborhood*

Philip Zimbardo's
The Lucifer Effect

Macat analyses are available from all good bookshops and libraries.

Access hundreds of analyses through one, multimedia tool.
Join free for one month **library.macat.com**

Macat Disciplines

Access the greatest ideas and thinkers across entire disciplines, including

Postcolonial Studies

Roland Barthes's *Mythologies*
Frantz Fanon's *Black Skin, White Masks*
Homi K. Bhabha's *The Location of Culture*
Gustavo Gutiérrez's *A Theology of Liberation*
Edward Said's *Orientalism*
Gayatri Chakravorty Spivak's *Can the Subaltern Speak?*

Macat analyses are available from all good bookshops and libraries.

Access hundreds of analyses through one, multimedia tool.
Join free for one month **library.macat.com**

Macat Disciplines

Access the greatest ideas and thinkers across entire disciplines, including

GLOBALIZATION

Arjun Appadurai's, *Modernity at Large: Cultural Dimensions of Globalisation*

James Ferguson's, *The Anti-Politics Machine*

Geert Hofstede's, *Culture's Consequences*

Amartya Sen's, *Development as Freedom*

Macat analyses are available from all good bookshops and libraries.

Access hundreds of analyses through one, multimedia tool.
Join free for one month **library.macat.com**

Macat Pairs

Analyse historical and modern issues from opposite sides of an argument. Pairs include:

HOW TO RUN AN ECONOMY

John Maynard Keynes's
The General Theory OF Employment, Interest and Money

Classical economics suggests that market economies are self-correcting in times of recession or depression, and tend toward full employment and output. But English economist John Maynard Keynes disagrees.

In his ground-breaking 1936 study *The General Theory*, Keynes argues that traditional economics has misunderstood the causes of unemployment. Employment is not determined by the price of labor; it is directly linked to demand. Keynes believes market economies are by nature unstable, and so require government intervention. Spurred on by the social catastrophe of the Great Depression of the 1930s, he sets out to revolutionize the way the world thinks

Milton Friedman's
The Role of Monetary Policy

Friedman's 1968 paper changed the course of economic theory. In just 17 pages, he demolished existing theory and outlined an effective alternate monetary policy designed to secure 'high employment, stable prices and rapid growth.'

Friedman demonstrated that monetary policy plays a vital role in broader economic stability and argued that economists got their monetary policy wrong in the 1950s and 1960s by misunderstanding the relationship between inflation and unemployment. Previous generations of economists had believed that governments could permanently decrease unemployment by permitting inflation—and vice versa. Friedman's most original contribution was to show that this supposed trade-off is an illusion that only works in the short term.

Macat Disciplines

Access the greatest ideas and thinkers across entire disciplines, including

THE FUTURE OF DEMOCRACY

Robert A. Dahl's, *Democracy and Its Critics*
Robert A. Dahl's, *Who Governs?*
Alexis De Toqueville's, *Democracy in America*
Niccolò Machiavelli's, *The Prince*
John Stuart Mill's, *On Liberty*
Robert D. Putnam's, *Bowling Alone*
Jean-Jacques Rousseau's, *The Social Contract*
Henry David Thoreau's, *Civil Disobedience*

Macat Disciplines

Access the greatest ideas and thinkers across entire disciplines, including

TOTALITARIANISM

Sheila Fitzpatrick's, *Everyday Stalinism*
Ian Kershaw's, *The "Hitler Myth"*
Timothy Snyder's, *Bloodlands*

Macat Pairs

Analyse historical and modern issues from opposite sides of an argument. Pairs include:

RACE AND IDENTITY

Zora Neale Hurston's
Characteristics of Negro Expression

Using material collected on anthropological expeditions to the South, Zora Neale Hurston explains how expression in African American culture in the early twentieth century departs from the art of white America. At the time, African American art was often criticized for copying white culture. For Hurston, this criticism misunderstood how art works. European tradition views art as something fixed. But Hurston describes a creative process that is alive, ever-changing, and largely improvisational. She maintains that African American art works through a process called 'mimicry'—where an imitated object or verbal pattern, for example, is reshaped and altered until it becomes something new, novel—and worthy of attention.

Frantz Fanon's
Black Skin, White Masks

Black Skin, White Masks offers a radical analysis of the psychological effects of colonization on the colonized.

Fanon witnessed the effects of colonization first hand both in his birthplace, Martinique, and again later in life when he worked as a psychiatrist in another French colony, Algeria. His text is uncompromising in form and argument. He dissects the dehumanizing effects of colonialism, arguing that it destroys the native sense of identity, forcing people to adapt to an alien set of values—including a core belief that they are inferior. This results in deep psychological trauma.

Fanon's work played a pivotal role in the civil rights movements of the 1960s.

Macat analyses are available from all good bookshops and libraries.

Access hundreds of analyses through one, multimedia tool.
Join free for one month **library.macat.com**

Macat Pairs

Analyse historical and modern issues from opposite sides of an argument. Pairs include:

INTERNATIONAL RELATIONS IN THE 21ST CENTURY

Samuel P. Huntington's
The Clash of Civilisations

In his highly influential 1996 book, Huntington offers a vision of a post-Cold War world in which conflict takes place not between competing ideologies but between cultures. The worst clash, he argues, will be between the Islamic world and the West: the West's arrogance and belief that its culture is a "gift" to the world will come into conflict with Islam's obstinacy and concern that its culture is under attack from a morally decadent "other."

Clash inspired much debate between different political schools of thought. But its greatest impact came in helping define American foreign policy in the wake of the 2001 terrorist attacks in New York and Washington.

Francis Fukuyama's
The End of History and the Last Man

Published in 1992, *The End of History and the Last Man* argues that capitalist democracy is the final destination for all societies. Fukuyama believed democracy triumphed during the Cold War because it lacks the "fundamental contradictions" inherent in communism and satisfies our yearning for freedom and equality. Democracy therefore marks the endpoint in the evolution of ideology, and so the "end of history." There will still be "events," but no fundamental change in ideology.

Macat analyses are available from all good bookshops and libraries.

Access hundreds of analyses through one, multimedia tool.
Join free for one month **library.macat.com**

Printed in the United States
by Baker & Taylor Publisher Services